OXFORD SLAVONIC PAPERS

Edited by

C. M. MACROBERT G. S. SMITH

and

G. C. STONE

General Editor

NEW SERIES

VOLUME XXVI

CLARENDON PRESS · OXFORD

1993

Oxford University Press, Walton Street, Oxford OX2 6DP
Oxford New York Toronto
Delhi Bombay Calcutta Madras Karachi
Kuala Lumpur Singapore Hong Kong Tokyo
Nairobi Dar es Salaam Cape Town
Melbourne Auckland Madrid
and associated companies in
Berlin Ibadan

Oxford is a trade mark of Oxford University Press

Published in the United States
by Oxford University Press Inc., New York

British Library Cataloguing in Publication Data
Data available

Library of Congress Cataloging in Publication Data
Data available
ISBN 0-19-815671-5

Typeset by Joshua Associates Ltd., Oxford
Printed in Great Britain
on acid-free paper by
Bookcraft (Bath) Ltd.
Midsomer Norton, Avon

THE editorial policy of the New Series of *Oxford Slavonic Papers* in general follows that of the original series, thirteen volumes of which appeared between the years 1950 and 1967. It is devoted to the publication of original contributions and documents relating to the languages, literatures, culture, and history of Russia and the other Slavonic countries, and appears annually. Reviews of individual books are not normally included, but bibliographical and review articles are published from time to time.

The British System of Cyrillic transliteration (British Standard 2979: 1958) has been adopted, omitting diacritics and using -y to express -й, -ий, -ій, and -ый at the end of personal names, e.g. Sergey, Dostoevsky, Bely, Grozny. For philological work the International System (ISO R/9) is used.

Editorial correspondence and typescripts should be addressed to Dr G. C. Stone at Hertford College, Oxford. Copies of the rules for style and presentation of typescripts will be supplied on request.

C. M. MACROBERT
G. S. SMITH
G. C. STONE

Hertford College, Oxford

CONTENTS

A Preliminary Comparison of the Curzon and Banica Gospels

By C. VAKARELIYSKA

THIS preliminary study offers a general introduction to British Library Add. MS 39628, a West Bulgarian tetraevangelion. For want of an established identifying title I shall refer to this manuscript as the Curzon Gospel (abbreviated as Cur) after Robert Curzon (1810–73), fourteenth Baron Zouche, who brought it to England from Mt. Athos in 1837. With the exception of the palaeographical samples in a table to a general study of fourteenth century Bulgarian palaeography[1] and several brief catalogue entries[2] I have found no mention of this manuscript in the scholarly literature. This lack of attention is an inevitable consequence of the manuscript's recent history, which is set forth in section 1 below.

Unlike many other Church Slavonic manuscripts, the Curzon Gospel can be reliably dated: the first year in its tables giving the dates of Sexagesima and Easter (as Cleminson notes)[3] is 1354 and, since the tables appear to be in the hand of the original primary scribe, this can be reasonably assumed to be approximately the

I am very grateful to Professor Horace G. Lunt, Dr C. M. MacRobert, and Professor David J. Birnbaum for many invaluable comments and suggestions on various drafts of this article. At the same time I remain fully responsible for all errors of contents and judgement. I also wish to thank Mr Julian Conway, Superintendent of Manuscripts, Mr A. E. Parker, Senior Conservation Officer for Western Manuscripts, and the staff of the Manuscript Department of the British Library for their assistance and co-operation over an extended period. The research for this article was made possible by a 1991 Georgetown University Summer Faculty Research Grant.

[1] Ž. Mištenko, 'Njakoi osobenosti na Tărnovskija ustav ot XIV v.', *Palaeobulgarica*, ix (1986), no. 1, pp. 6–19.

[2] British Museum, *Catalogue of Additions to the Manuscripts, 20 (1916–1920)*, (London, 1933), 101; A. Djourova and I. Dujčev, *Slavonic Manuscripts from the British Museum and Library* (London, 1978), 25; A. Džurova and I. Dujčev, *Slavjanski răkopisi ot Britanskija Muzej i Biblioteka* (Sofia, 1977), 25; A. Džurova, *1000 godini bălgarska răkopisna kniga* (Sofia, 1981), plate 151; K. Kuev, *Sădbata na starobălgarskata răkopisna kniga prez vekovete*, 1 ed. (Sofia, 1979), 54; 2 ed. (Sofia, 1986), 58–9; R. Cleminson (comp.), *The Anne Pennington Catalogue. A Union Catalogue of Cyrillic Manuscripts in British and Irish Collections* (London, 1988), 123.

[3] Cleminson, *Pennington Catalogue* (n. 2), 123.

year in which the manuscript was written[4]. As a datable manuscript, the Curzon Gospel provides a chronological framework both for the study of its own palaeographic, orthographic, and linguistic features, and for the comparative analysis of other medieval Bulgarian gospel manuscripts. The focus of this article is the significance of the Curzon Gospel as a source of information on the Banica Gospel, another West Bulgarian tetraevangelion[5].

The Banica Gospel (abbreviated as Ban) has been attributed by specialists in Bulgaria to the thirteenth century,[6] but this dating has been put into question by Lunt's observation that the palaeographic features of the manuscript appear more typical of the middle or of the second half of the fourteenth century.[7] The potential of the Curzon Gospel to resolve this issue lies in its unusual relationship to the Banica Gospel: striking coincidences between the two manuscripts, which include identically located syntactic errors, lexical anomalies, and repetitions and omissions of text, indicate that the Curzon Gospel and Banica Gospel versions of Mark, Luke, and John were copied either from a single manuscript or from two very closely related manuscripts. (It is highly unlikely that either manuscript was copied from the other, since each contains numerous omissions of standard text that the other preserves.) Whereas in the Banica Gospel parts of Luke and John (Luke 16: 14–17: 2, 17: 24–18: 9, 21: 7–22: 12, and John 10: 41–11: 25, 11: 47–12: 10, 16: 30–17: 17, 19: 7–27) are missing, the text of these portions is intact in the Curzon Gospel. By close examination and comparison of the versions of Mark, Luke, and John in both manuscripts it should be possible to determine more

[4] The manuscript is also attributed to the fourteenth century by Kuev, *Sădbata* (n. 2), 1 ed. (1979), 54; 2 ed. (1986), 58. Cf. a more approximate dating to the thirteenth or fourteenth century by Djourova and Dujčev, *Slavonic Manuscripts* (n. 2), 25, Džurova, *1000 godini* (n. 2), plate 151, and Mištenko, 'Njakoi osobenosti' (n. 1), attached table.

[5] Published by E. Dogramadžieva and B. Rajkov, *Baniško evangelie* (Sofia, 1981). This manuscript was first described in I. Momčilov, *Sbornik ot obrazci za izučavaneto na starobălgarskija ezik po sičkoto mu razvitie* (Vienna, 1865), 12–20, 43–6, and was analysed as the 'Pop Ioan' Gospel in B. Conev, 'Knižovni starini ot Elena', *Godišnik na Sofijskija universitet. Istoriko-filologičeski fakultet*, xix (1923), no. 7, pp. 1–33.

[6] Conev, 'Knižovni starini' (n. 5), 4; a late thirteenth-century dating is given in Momčilov, *Sbornik ot obrazci* (n. 5), 14; M. Stojanov and X. Kodov, *Opis na slavjanskite răkopisi v Sofijskata Narodna Biblioteka* (Sofia, 1964), 18; Džurova, *1000 godini* (n. 2), 96 and plate 123; Dogramadžieva and Rajkov, *Baniško evangelie* (n. 5), 68; and B. Xristova, D. Karadžova, and A. Ikonomova, *Bălgarski răkopisi ot XI do XVII vek zapazeni v Bălgaria. Svoden katalog*, i (Sofia, 1982), 34.

[7] H. G. Lunt, 'On Editing Early Slavic Manuscripts: The Case of the Codex Suprasliensis, the Mstislav Gospel, and the Banica Gospel', *International Journal of Slavic Linguistics and Poetics*, xxx (1984), 7–76 (esp. 59–60).

accurately which of the textual and linguistic idiosyncrasies in each of them can be attributed to each scribe and which to an earlier shared source. It is also possible that further information pertinent to the date and geographic origin of both manuscripts will be found in the full menology in the Curzon Gospel, which, with the exception of differences in the names of individual saints listed for particular days, is similar to the Banica menology in form and content.

Section 1 below provides an account of the recent history of the Curzon Gospel, section 2 a brief description of its physical composition, palaeographic features, and orthography. Section 3 focuses on the Curzon and Banica versions of Mark, Luke, and John, presenting examples of textual coincidences between these two manuscripts within the context of the general transmission tradition which they share with the earlier Dobrejšo Gospel, and against the background of approximately contemporaneous Bulgarian Church Slavonic gospel manuscripts, as well as canonical Old Church Slavonic (hereafter OCS) gospels. The Curzon Gospel version of Matthew is discussed briefly in section 4. It should be emphasized that my findings are published at an early stage in a long-term project and are preliminary in nature.

1

The Curzon Gospel is one of several Bulgarian and Serbian Church Slavonic manuscripts that were acquired by Robert Curzon during his travels in the Levant in 1837. The best known of these is the illuminated Tsar Ivan Alexander Gospel (also known as the London Gospel).[8] The Curzon Gospel, which lacks its first and last few pages, including the colophon, if there ever was one, was kept in Curzon's private collection of manuscripts and writing materials at his estate at Parham until 19 April 1876, three years after his death, when at least part of the private collection known as the Parham Collection was placed on loan to the British Museum.[9] However, the Museum did not catalogue the items until the entire Parham Collection came into its ownership in 1917 as a bequest of

[8] British Library Add. MS 39627. Curzon's record of his travels includes an entertaining account of his encounter with the Tsar Ivan Alexander Gospel on Mt. Athos. See his *Visits to Monasteries in the Levant* (London, 1849), 422–4; reprint (London, 1955), 328–30.

[9] There is a note to this effect on a flyleaf in Curzon's hand-notated copy of the private catalogue to the collection (British Library Add. MS 64098, fol. 1).

Curzon's daughter Darea, Baroness Zouche.[10] The Parham Collection was not included in the Museum's published catalogue until 1933.[11] The absence of any mention of the Curzon Gospel in the nineteenth and early twentieth-century descriptions of Slavonic manuscripts at the British Museum[12] suggests that it was not among those manuscripts from the Parham Collection that were placed on loan with the Museum in 1876. This is not surprising, since unlike the visually spectacular Tsar Ivan Alexander Gospel, which is the focal point of each of these descriptions, the Curzon Gospel is an aesthetically unappealing manuscript, written on poor-quality vellum and in some places around gaping holes, devoid of all but the simplest graphic ornamentation, and containing many erasures, crossings-out, and alterations by several later hands. Unexpected, however, is the absence of the Curzon Gospel from Gudev's 1892 descriptions of the Bulgarian manuscripts in the Parham Collection when it was still in private hands.[13]

This omission is due to the fact that the descriptions are based

[10] British Museum, *Catalogue* (n. 2), 101; DNB, s. v. 'Curzon'; see also F. Uspenskij, 'O nekotoryx slavjanskix i po slavjanski pisannyx rukopisjax, xranjaščixsja v Londone i Oksforde', *Žurnal Ministerstva narodnogo prosveščenija*, 1878, č. cxcix(2), pp. 1–21, č. cc(2), pp. 63–94. These facts are somewhat garbled in Gudev's description of the Tsar Ivan Alexander Gospel, which gives the title 'Lord Zouche' to Curzon's son, while referring to Robert Curzon himself as 'Lord Curzon' (P. T. Gudev, 'Bălgarski răkopisi v bibliotekata na lord Zouche', *Sbornik za narodni umotvorenija, nauka i knižnina*, vii (1892) 159–223; viii (1892), 137–68 (esp. vii (162)). This error is repeated in B. Conev, *Istorija na bălgarskija ezik*, 1 ed. (Sofia, 1919), 235, and 2 ed. (Sofia, 1984), 196, and in I. Talev, *Some Problems of the Second South Slavic Influence in Russian* (Munich, 1973), 201. Actually, both father and son at some point during their lives were titled Lord Zouche or, alternatively, Lord de la Zouche (see DNB, s. v. 'Curzon'). A grandson of the first Viscount Curzon, Robert Curzon was officially 'the Hon. Robert Curzon' at the time of the first publication of his works referring to the Tsar Ivan Alexander Gospel; in 1870, three years before his death, he succeeded his mother to the Barony of Zouche and became the fourteenth Baron Zouche. On his death the barony passed to his son Robin (d. 1914), who became the fifteenth Baron Zouche. See I. H. C. Fraser, *The Heir of Parham: Robert Curzon, Fourteenth Baron Zouche* (London, 1986), xiv. Talev (op. cit., 201) confuses the name of Curzon's estate with the surname of his heir and states incorrectly that the collection was bequeathed to the Museum in the 1920s by 'the widow of Lord Parham' [*sic*]. For a more accurate account of Curzon's acquisition of the Tsar Ivan Alexander Gospel, see B. Filov, 'Londonskoto evangelie na Ivan Aleksandra i negovite miniatjuri', *Spisanie na BAN. Klon istoriko-filologičen i filosofsko-obštestven*, xxxviii (1929), no. 20, pp. 1–32.

[11] British Museum, *Catalogue* (n. 2), nos. 39583–39671.

[12] I. Sreznevskij, 'Slavjanskie rukopisi Britanskogo muzeja v Londone i Bodlejskoj biblioteki v Oksforde', *Izvestija Imperatorskogo arxeologičeskogo obščestva*, 1872 no. 7(3), pp. 233–5; Uspenskij, op. cit. (n. 10); V. Jagič, 'Slavica im British Museum', *Archiv für slavische Philologie*, vi (1882), 617–18; K. Grot, 'Londonskie zametki: Slavjanskie rukopisi Britanskogo muzeja. Slavistika v Anglii', *Russkij filologičeskij vestnik*, 1887 no. 17, pp. 1–29; P. A. Syrku, 'Slavjanskie i russkie rukopisi Britanskogo muzeja v Londone', *Sbornik Otdelenija russkogo jazyka i slovesnosti Imperatorskoj Akademii nauk*, lxxxiv (1908) no. 4, pp. iii–xv, 1–86.

[13] Gudev, 'Bălgarski răkopisi' (n. 10).

on the listings in Curzon's private catalogue, printed in fifty copies in 1849,[14] which does not purport to be an exhaustive listing of all the manuscripts in the Parham Collection. On the contrary, both its printed preface and Curzon's handwritten preface to his own copy, which was given to the Museum as part of the bequest, state explicitly that it lists only a portion of the manuscripts at Parham.[15]

Curzon's private catalogue describes under the heading 'Bulgarian' four manuscripts, three of which can readily be identified with manuscripts that are now in the British Library.[16] These are no. 151, a blue-bound fourteenth-century Bulgarian Church Slavonic gospel;[17] no. 152, a red-bound illuminated Serbian Church Slavonic gospel;[18] and no. 153, the Tsar Ivan Alexander Gospel. No. 150 in the catalogue is described as a copy of the Acts and Epistles, bound in brown velvet and 'not quite perfect'. On the basis of firsthand examination of the Parham manuscripts lent to the British Museum in 1876, both Grot and Uspenskij reported the absence of a manuscript fitting this description.[19] Nor is any manuscript corresponding to the description of no. 150 listed in the British Museum catalogue, the Pennington catalogue, or the Djourova and Dujčev catalogue. The

[14] R. Curzon, *Catalogue of Materials for Writing, Early Writings on Tablets and Stones, Rolled and Other Manuscripts and Oriental Manuscript Books at Parham in the County of Somerset* (London, 1849).

[15] 'The present Catalogue contains a description of some Manuscripts, which form part of a Collection made principally in the Levant and on the continent of Europe' (ibid. 6). Cf. Gudev's assertion ('Bălgarski răkopisi' (n. 10), vii. 159) that the private catalogue includes all the items in the Parham Collection. The handwritten preface to Curzon's own annotated copy of the printed private catalogue (British Library Add. MS 64098, fol. 4) indicates that the number of items in the collection well exceeded the number of catalogue entries: 'I wish to reduce my collection to the smallest bounds possible, and therefore have divided it, into three principal heads; each of which I am desirous of limiting to about 200 specimens, which will I think be sufficient to give some notion of the different contrivances by which mankind has been enabled to transmit their ideas to one another and to preserve the rewards of distant age, for the benefit of generations yet unborn.' This statement is confirmed by a handwritten note attached to Curzon's copy of the catalogue, which tabulates the various types of items in the collection, arriving at a total of 284 items (ibid., fol. 2^v). Evidence that the Museum received as part of the bequest certain manuscripts that are not accounted for in Curzon's private catalogue is provided by the later annotations made by Museum staff regarding certain manuscripts from the collection. These annotations, which now compose fols. 95–96 of Curzon's own copy of the private catalogue, correlate the Museum's own acquisition numbers to Curzon's catalogue numbers; some of the acquisition numbers are left unmatched and followed by question marks.

[16] Curzon, *Catalogue* (n. 14), 18. The manuscript holdings of the British Museum were transferred to the British Library in 1973.

[17] British Library Add. MS 39625.

[18] British Library Add. MS 39626.

[19] Grot, 'Londonskie zametki' (n. 12), 1–2; Uspenskij, op. cit. (n. 10), 1.

description of the Curzon Gospel in the British Museum catalogue, however, does comment on its physical similarity to no. 150:[20] 'On f.i. is written no. 236, but the book corresponds in outward appearance to Bulgarian MSS. no. 1, p. 31 of the *Curzon Cat.*, which, however, is described as containing the Acts and Epistles (pencil numbering 150).' Apparently using this tentative observation as a starting-point, Djourova and Dujčev confidently identify no. 150 with the Curzon Gospel.[21] It is extremely unlikely, however, that the Curzon Gospel is the manuscript listed as no. 150 in Curzon's catalogue. First, Curzon's catalogue contains only 200 entries, yet the British Museum catalogue notes that fol. i of the Curzon Gospel bears the registry mark 236; this circumstance in itself probably indicates that the manuscript was from a part of the Parham Collection not listed in the private catalogue. Secondly, by no stretch of the imagination can the bright crimson velvet cover of the Curzon Gospel be described as brown;[22] moreover, although it is not known whom Curzon consulted in compiling the description of the Slavonic manuscripts in his catalogue, it is extremely hard to believe that any individual capable of identifying as gospels the other three Slavonic manuscripts listed there would have failed to recognize this one, let alone mistake it for the Acts and Epistles. Finally, and most obviously, the severe damage to the upper portion of fols. 1–42 and the absence of a number of folios (including the first five chapters of Matthew) hardly fit Curzon's description of no. 150 as 'not quite perfect'.

That British Library Add. MS 39628 was indeed one of the items

[20] British Museum, *Catalogue* (n. 2), 101.

[21] Djourova and Dujčev, *Slavonic Manuscripts* (n. 2), 25. Cf. the more careful wording in Kuev, *Sădbata* (n. 2), 1 ed. (1979), 54 and 2 ed. (1986), 58–9. The account in Djourova and Dujčev states that the registry number 236 appears on 'f. 1r', i.e. on the first page of the Matthew text; this information is repeated by Kuev. The Museum's specification of fol. i (British Museum, *Catalogue* (n. 2), 101) is more likely, as this folio, which is made of vellum of a much later date, was added to the manuscript during the binding process and forms the pastedown to the inside front cover. There appears to be an erasure in the lower right corner of fol. i, although no registry number 236 is now visible on the manuscript even under video spectral analysis. It is also possible, alternatively, that the newer vellum folio now marked 'fol. i' was inserted by the Museum to replace an original folio bearing the registry number when the cover was removed and recased in 1927 (A. E. Parker, Senior Conservation Officer for Western Manuscripts, personal communication).

[22] While it is possible, of course, that the volume was rebound at some time after Curzon's catalogue was published (and Museum records do show that the manuscript was at the bindery in 1927 and again in 1977), the crimson covering apparently pre-dates the Museum acquisition, as it was not the Museum's practice to bind in velvet. (Add. MS 38625, another fourteenth-century Bulgarian gospel manuscript from the Parham Collection, bears a blue velvet cover; Uspenskij's physical description of this manuscript (op. cit. (n. 10), 2), listed as no. 151 in Curzon's catalogue, is incorrect. Grot, 'Londonskie zametki' (n. 12), 2, draws attention to Uspenskij's error.)

brought to England by Robert Curzon is established by its listing in the Museum catalogue as part of the bequest of Lady Zouche. In any event, whether it was miscatalogued as 'Acts and Epistles' or simply left uncatalogued for nearly one hundred years, the obscurity of the Curzon Gospel is the result of its virtual inaccessibility until publication of the Djourova and Dujčev catalogue in 1978.

2

A detailed physical description of the Curzon Gospel can be found in the Pennington catalogue.[23] The text begins at Matt. 6: 14, after which the remainder of Matthew is intact; this is followed by intact texts of Mark (fols. 44^{r}–75^{v}), Luke (fols. 75^{v}–130^{v}), and John (fols. 130^{v}–172^{v}). The manuscript contains a full menology that begins on the last page of John (fols. 172^{v}–185^{v}), followed by two synaxaria (fols. 185^{v}–194^{v}, 194^{v}–196^{r}), and Sexagesima and Easter tables for the years 1354 to 1492 inclusive (fols. 196^{r}–198^{v}). Since each of these calendars begins on the last page of the text that precedes it, rather than on a new folio, they all can be assumed to have formed part of the original manuscript. In general, the menology is similar to that of the Banica Gospel in content, but there are some differences in form, as the Banica menology frequently adds alleluias and other liturgical instructions that are not found in the corresponding text in the Curzon Gospel. There are also occasional divergences in the names of saints listed both for specific dates and for series of dates (for example, 8–24 April, Cur fols. 181^{v}–182^{r}), which may perhaps provide some further information on the dates and origins of both manuscripts. Each of the manuscripts also contains a pair of synaxaria. While the second synaxaria have little in common, the first synaxaria are similar in both form and content.

The manuscript is written in a small semi-uncial hand in black ink, with very rudimentary and sparse ornamentation. Liturgical rubrics and some verse-initial letters of the Gospel text are written in red ink of an orangish shade; the initial letters to entries in the menology are generally also in red ink. The pages consist of 26 lines, with the exception of fols. 128^{r}–129^{v}, which contain 28 lines (see below), fol. 34^{r}–34^{v}, which contains 23 lines because of defects in the vellum, fols. 104^{r}–107^{v}, which contain 25 lines, fols.

[23] Cleminson, *Pennington Catalogue* (n. 2), 123.

140[r]–143[r], which contain 27 lines, and isolated folios, particularly in the menology, which contain a partial or full 27th line to accommodate spill-over text or liturgical rubrics (fols. 7[v], 37[v], 39[v], 57[v], 127[r], 151[v], 173[r], 174[v], 175[r], 176[r], 176[v], 182[r], 190[v], 192[v], 193[r], 193[v], 198[v]); the top few lines of fols. 1–42 are fully or partially illegible as a result of water damage.[24]

The entire manuscript appears to have been copied by a single scribe,[25] with the exception of Matt. 23: 6 (fol. 31[r]), where a more elegant contemporaneous hand has contributed the first eight lines of the page; this secondary hand ends in the middle of l. 8, where the text is picked up immediately in the primary hand. It can be said at this preliminary juncture that the primary hand is characterized by the distinctive shape of the letter **ү** which forms a c-shape at the juncture with the stem, by the rightward-sloping tail of the letter **щ**, and by the rightward slant of the letters **а** and **ꙗ**. These features are also present in the menology and synaxaria, although the lettering is cramped and the spacing narrower, apparently as a result of attempts to leave space for the many red initial letters that were added in the same hand after the rest of the text had been written in black. The secondary hand is more similar to the hand of the primary Banica scribe, although not identical: the letters are rounded, but curve downward toward the right; vowel letters that are word-initial or preceded by another vowel are marked by the same sort of diacritics as in the Banica Gospel, but points are centred high, as in the hand of the primary scribe.

Folios 128[r]–129[v] contain 28 lines rather than the usual 26, and, as a result of careless ruling, the text of fols. 128[r] and 129[r] slopes noticeably upward to the right; fols. 128[v] and 129[v] correspondingly slope downward, in contrast to the rest of the folios. The text of fol. 129[v] ends in the middle of line 27 and is picked up immediately, without gaps or repetition, by the 26-line text on fol. 130[r]; this, together with the fact that the insert appears in the only gathering that contains eight rather than six folios, suggests that the insert was intended to replace omitted text rather than lost folios. The hand of the insert is noticeably larger and untidier than that of the rest of the manuscript, the letters being spaced further

[24] While the running of ink and puckering on these pages is indeed evidence of water damage, the possibility of there having been additional fire damage is not to be excluded. Infra-red analysis of the damaged folios indicates the presence of a small degree of carbon that may have been caused either by burning or by water contact with the ink, which is carbon-based.

[25] Palaeographic samples of the manuscript appear in Djourova and Dujčev, *Slavonic Manuscripts* (n. 2), plates 1–3, and in the table attached to Mištenko, 'Njakoi osobenosti' (n. 1).

apart and of less uniform height. The liturgical instructions are written in red ink of a bluer shade than the red-orange cinnabar colour used on the other folios; infra-red analysis confirms that the red is of a different composition, but indicates that the black ink is of the type used on the other folios. While the evidence is still inconclusive, the inserted folios appear to have been written by the primary scribe, as they exhibit the same unusual **ү** and characteristic rightward-slanting **щ** and **а**.

The manuscript has been corrected by a number of later hands. As noted in the Pennington catalogue,[26] fols. 1^{r}–8^{r} (Matt. 6: 14–11: 4) and 130^{v}–163^{v} (John 1: 1–16: 22) have been altered in brownish ink by an apparently later and definitely more uneven hand (referred to hereafter as 'corrector A') that has inserted omitted text and altered case-endings, spelling, and the location of verse numbers, as well as often changing lexicon and syntax to conform to a different textual tradition. These folios contain superscript accentuation marks in brown ink that can be assumed to have been added by this corrector, since they do not appear anywhere else; the altered Matthew folios also contain in some places what appear to be musical directions. A second, more flowing and elegant hand (hereafter 'corrector B') has also made occasional corrections in brown ink (although without adding diacritics), using a finer pen and minimizing the distinction between thick and thin strokes. These modifications appear to be confined primarily to Mark and Luke. Alterations also have been made to the menology and synaxaria by both these correctors and, apparently, by the secondary scribe, while the Sexagesima and Easter tables may have been altered by yet another hand. It appears in addition that other later hands have contributed occasional modifications throughout the manuscript. In most instances the original text is still legible under the alterations and erasures. The only remaining personal message in a hand at all similar to the original scribe's is the unevenly-written phrase **помози ми**, which appears in the lower margin of fol. 39^{r}.

The same basic orthographic system is used by both original scribes. There are a great many orthographic inconsistencies in the manuscript, however, that deserve closer study than has been possible so far. In general, it may be said that, like many West Bulgarian manuscripts, the Curzon Gospel uses a single-jer, single-jus system. With the exception of one unambiguous back jer (**възалка**, Matt 21: 18, fol. 27^{r}, 1. 26), all jers are represented by the letter **ь**. A double jer appears in Matt. 10: 34 (**мь|чьь**, fol. 7^{v}, ll. 22-

[26] Cleminson, *Pennington Catalogue* (n. 2), 123.

3). (In the extracts presented here and below, right margins are indicated by the symbol |, and right margins at page end by the symbol ||.) The letter **ѧ** represents both front and back jusy; the ambiguous letter **ꙛ** is occasionally substituted for **ѧ** after another vowel or in word-initial position: e.g Matt. 24: 30, fol. 34r, l. 6 **силоꙛ**; Luke 1: 52, fol. 77v, l. 22 **силныꙛ**; John 12: 43, fol. 156v, l. 24 **земнѧꙛ**; Mark 10: 33, fol. 62v, l. 26 **ꙛзыкомь**.[27] The letter **ꙛ** appears to occur most frequently and in its most clearly delineated form in Matthew and Mark, and is noticeably infrequent in John. Matthew is also the site of what appears to be an unambiguous **ѫ** in the original hand (Matt. 7: 27, fol. 3r, l. 25 **ѥѫ**). In addition, there are a few occurrences of ambiguous letters in Matthew and Mark that may be construed either as **ꙛ** or as **ѫ** (e.g. Matt. 18: 12, fol. 22r, l. 8 **заблѧжⷣьшѧꙛ**; Matt 19: 29, fol. 24v, l. 20 **братꙛ**; Mark 7: 35, fol. 56v, l. 24 **ꙛза**). In some places **ѧ** appears instead of expected **а**: e.g. **винѧ не имѧть** (John 2: 3, fol. 132v, l. 25, altered to neuter genitive singular **вина** by corrector A), **ѿ | страхѧ** (Matt. 14: 26, fol. 16r, ll. 7-8); in other places **а** appears where, in the orthographic system which the scribe is apparently trying to use, one would expect **ѧ** or **ѣ**: e.g. **прикоснашѧ** for **прикоснѧшѧ** (Matt. 14: 36, fol. 16v, l. 2), **зало** for **зѣло** (Mark 16: 2, fol. 74v, l. 18), **стражⷣащихь** for **страждѧщихь** (Luke 6: 18, fol. 88r, l. 5), **ѡсаждаите** for **ѡсѧждаите** (Luke 6: 37, fol. 89r, l. 1), **вьзмаⷮ** for **вьзмѧⷮ** (John 19: 31, fol. 169r, l. 26). There are also instances of **ѧ** where one would expect **ь** or **ꙗ**: e.g. **стѧзи** for **стьзѧ** (Mark 1: 3, fol. 44r, l. 19, also Ban **стѧзы**), **илиѧ** for nom. **илиꙗ** (John 1: 21, fol. 131r, l. 20); and **ѣ** where one would expect **ѧ**: e.g. **крьстѣщѧ** for **крьстѧщѧ** (Matt. 28: 19, fol. 44r, l. 9), **послѣ** for **послѧ** (Mark 1: 2, fol. 44r, l. 15), **смѧрить сѧ и | смѣрѣѧ сѧ** (Matt. 23: 12, fol. 31r, ll. 12-13). Dzělo is used only as a numeral. While most lines end in vowel letters, there are occasional examples of lines ending in consonants throughout the manuscript: e.g. **д|роугоѥ** (Matt. 13: 5, fol. 12r, ll. 16-17), **прѣп|рѧдѧ** (Mark 15: 20, fol. 73v, ll. 4-5), **ѥм|оу** (Luke 1: 11, fol. 76r, ll. 11-12), **п|риѧшѧ** (John 1: 11, fol. 130v, ll. 23-4).

The orthography of the menology and synaxaria differs from that of the gospels in what appears to be a considerably more frequent use of **є** for **ѥ** and **а** for **ꙗ** both in word-initial position and within a word, if they immediately follow another vowel letter: e.g. **оутрина**, fol. 189v, l. 23; **єдинь**, fol. 175v, l. 18. Moreover, the ambiguous letter **ꙛ** is absent from the menology and synaxaria; all jusy in the original primary hand are here represented by **ѧ**: e.g.

[27] Cf. the classification of this letter as **ѫ** in the table in Mištenko, 'Njakoi osobenosti' (n. 1).

с҃тиѧ. This may be compared with тобоѧ, a correction in what appears to be the hand of the secondary original scribe on fol. 173^{r}, l. 12. While these differences may be indications that the menology was written by a different scribe, the hand is not noticeably different. The orthography displays the usual confusion between а and ѧ in the nominative and accusative feminine singular and in the genitive masculine singular of nouns (e.g. masc. gen. маматиѧ, 2 September, fol. 173^{r}, l. 6; Ban маман'та), and initial vowel letters are occasionally omitted in personal names preceded by a word-final vowel: e.g. с҃томү милиꙗноү(19 July, fol. 184^{v}, l. 12; Ban с҃томꙋ емилианоү), и настаса (22 Jan., fol. 179^{v}, l. 6, Ban и анастаса).

3

The analysis below presents examples of lexical and textual coincidences between the Curzon and Banica Gospels, and compares shared items with their equivalents in other Bulgarian Church Slavonic and Old Church Slavonic gospels. The manuscripts used for comparative purposes are the Codex Zographensis (abbreviated as Zo);[28] the Codex Marianus (abbreviated as Mar), which contains more markedly western features than Zo;[29] the Dobrejšo Gospel (abbreviated as Dobrš), a West Bulgarian manuscript that is earlier than but comes from the same general textual tradition as Ban and Cur;[30] the Dobromir Gospel (abbreviated as Dbrm), a Macedonian manuscript (earlier than Ban and Cur) that contains elements of both the Marianus and Dobrejšo traditions;[31] and the contemporaneous Tsar Ivan

[28] Published by V. Jagić, *Quattuor evangeliorum Codex glagoliticus olim Zographensis nunc Petropolitanus* (Berlin, 1879) (photographic reprint, Graz, 1954).

[29] Published by V. Jagić, *Quattuor evangeliorum versionis palaeoslovenicae Codex Marianus glagoliticus* (Berlin, 1883) (photographic reprint, Graz, 1960).

[30] Published by B. Conev, *Dobrejšovo četveroevangele: Srednobălgarski pametnik ot XIII v.* (Bălgarski starini, i) (Sofia, 1906). On the common lexical tradition of the Dobrejšo and Banica Gospels, see N. V. Kossek, 'O leksike srednebolgarskix evangelij', *Palaeobulgarica*, viii (1984), no. 3, pp. 57–86. Most Bulgarian sources date the Dobrejšo Gospel to the thirteenth century (e.g. Kuev, *Sădbata* (n. 2), 1 ed. (1979), 176, 2 ed. (1986), 210; Džurova, *1000 godini* (n. 2), 126 (first half of the thirteenth century); Xristova, Karadžova, and Ikonomova (eds.), *Bălgarski răkopisi* (n. 6), 24 (first half of the thirteenth century); Conev, *Dobrejšovo četveroevangele,* 6 (early thirteenth century)). For the purposes of this article I shall reserve judgement on the accuracy of the dates proposed for all manuscripts other than the Curzon Gospel.

[31] Published in a photographic edition by M. Altbauer, *Dobromirovo evangelie: kirilski spomenik od XII vek* (Skopje, 1973) and in a printed edition by B. Velčeva, *Dobromirovo evangelie: bălgarski pametnik ot načaloto na XII vek* (Sofia, 1975). Nine recently discovered folios (Matt. 21:24-24:3, 27:48-62) are reproduced in I. C. Tarnanidis, *The Slavonic*

Alexander Gospel (abbreviated as IvAl),[32] an East Bulgarian tetraevangelion that bears the date 1356 and is textually somewhat closer to the Codex Marianus. The Dobromir and Dobrejšo manuscripts are imperfect and therefore do not always provide parallel passages for comparative purposes. As the Curzon and Banica Gospels show a certain degree of lectionary influence, equivalent passages from the Codex Assemanianus (abbreviated as Ass)[33] and two Bulgarian Church Slavonic lectionary gospels, the Koxno Gospel (abbreviated as Kox)[34] and the Plovdiv Gospel (abbreviated as Plov),[35] are also provided, where available.[36]

Many of the discrepancies between the Curzon and Banica excerpts presented below (e.g. in the spelling of foreign words, particle usage, and the distribution of past participles and aorists and of long- and short-form adjectives) are, of course, quite common in Bulgarian Church Slavonic manuscripts and do not in themselves provide evidence concerning the protograph. Certain other anomalies in the Curzon Gospel excerpts are interesting in their own right, but the analysis here is confined primarily to those

Manuscripts Discovered in 1975 on Mount Sinai (Thessaloniki, 1988), 202-3, 317-34 (photographic edition). The Dobromir Gospel is generally considered to date from the twelfth century. See V. Jagić, *Evangelium Dobromiri: Ein altmacedonisches Denkmal der kirchenslavischen Sprache des XII. Jahrhunderts* (Sitzungsberichte der kaiserlichen Akademie der Wissenschaften in Wien: Philosophisch-historische Classe, cxxxviii (1897 (1898)), Abhandlung 2, and cxl (1899), Abhandlung 3), cxxxvii (1897 (1898)), Abhandlung 2, pp. 4, 7; Altbauer, *Dobromirovo*, xiii. An early twelfth-century dating has been proposed by Velčeva, *Dobromirovo evangelie*, 17–23; see also Kuev, *Sădbata* (n. 2), 1 ed. (1979), 164, 2 ed. (1986), 199. On lectionary contamination in the Dobromir Gospel, see Jagić, *Evangelium Dobromiri*, cxl (1899), Abhandlung 3, pp. 4, 114.

[32] British Library Add. MS 39627. L.Živkova, *Četveroevangelieto na car Ivan Aleksandăr* (Sofia, 1980) provides legible facsimiles only of illuminated pages.

[33] Published by J. Kurz, *Evangeliarum Assemani: Codex Vaticanus 3, Slavicus glagoliticus*, ii (Prague, 1955).

[34] N.V. Kossek proposes a late thirteenth-century dating for this manuscript. See her photographic edition, *Evangelie Koxno* (Sofia, 1986), 7.

[35] G.M. Michel in his hand-copied edition, *Das Plovdiver Evangeliar*, Slavische Sprachen und Literaturen, Band 14 (Neuried, 1987), p. vi, dates the manuscript to the late thirteenth or early fourteenth century.

[36] Extracts from the Curzon Gospel and the Tsar Ivan Alexander Gospel are here reproduced from the manuscripts. Other extracts are quoted from Dogramadžieva and Rajkov, *Baniško evangelie* (n. 5); Jagić, *Codex Zographensis* (n.28); Jagić, *Codex Marianus* (n. 29); Conev, *Dobrejšovo četveroevangele* (n. 30); Altbauer, *Dobromirovo evangelie* (n. 31) (using Velčeva, *Dobromirovo evangelie* (n. 31) to clarify illegible portions); Kurz, *Evangeliarum Assemani* (n. 33); Kossek, *Evangelie Koxno* (n. 34); and Michel, *Plovdiver Evangeliar* (n. 35). Except in Table 1 below, which contains normalized forms, where more than one manuscript reference is given for any quotation of text, the text is reproduced as it appears in the first manuscript listed. Unless otherwise indicated, lexical items and textual excerpts shared by the Curzon Gospel with other manuscripts are reproduced as they appear in the Curzon Gospel. Ligatures, stress marks, dots over initial vowels, and other diacritics are not shown; superscript letters are not necessarily reproduced in the locations in which they appear in the manuscripts. Additions or corrections by later hands are not

repetitions, omissions, and lexical and syntactic coincidences between the Curzon Gospel and the Banica Gospel that do not appear either in the Dobrejšo Gospel (which clearly shares a common original protograph with both manuscripts for Mark, Luke, and John) or in any other Bulgarian Church Slavonic gospels that I have so far examined. Of particular interest are the usually parallel placement and content of the liturgical rubrics in the two texts, an example of which appears below. Orthographic discrepancies, the alternation of participles and finite verbs and of older and newer morphological forms, and the presence or absence of the conjunction и and of personal pronouns are, for the purposes of this article, not treated as significant.

The close relationship of the Banica, Curzon, and Dobrejšo versions of Mark, Luke, and John is illustrated in part by the sample lexical coincidences presented in Table 1 below, which have been selected on the basis of Jagić's, Horálek's,[37] and, to a lesser extent, Slavova's[38] lexical lists. All the entries from Slavova's list that are shared by the Dobrejšo and Banica Gospels in Mark, Luke, and John also occur in identical locations in the Curzon Gospel. (In John, in all three manuscripts, there is an abrupt general change just before chapter 12 from West Bulgarian to East Bulgarian lexicon).[39] Also included in Table 1 are some of the more noteworthy entries from Dogramadžieva's lexical list for the Banica Gospel,[40] as well as several additional items not included in any of the four lists mentioned. The table lists occurrences of lexical items that the Banica and Curzon Gospels have in common

included in the reproduction of the texts, but are discussed in the accompanying notes. Abbreviations that appear in the published texts without superscript letters are marked with a titlo: e.g. г҃и. Word divisions have occasionally been adjusted for conformity. In particular, the word divisions in Conev, *Dobrejšovo četveroevangele* (n. 30) have been adjusted by inserting a space between host words and their clitics. Right-hand margins are not marked in extracts from the Dobrejšo Gospel, as they are not shown in Conev's edition. Liturgical instructions are enclosed in curly brackets { }, letters written in red ink are underlined. Angle brackets < > enclose letters erased in the manuscript. The symbol <...> indicates an omission of text on the part of the scribe, while [...] represents the omission of words by the author of this article. Illegible letters are indicated by <--->.

[37] V. Jagič, *Entstehungsgeschichte der altkirchenslavischen Sprache* (Vienna, 1913), 281–421; idem, *Evangelium Dobromiri*, cxl (1899), Abhandlung 3, pp. 4–51; K. Horálek, *Evangeliáře a čtveroevangelia: Příspěvky k textové kritice a k dějinám staroslověnského překladu evangelia* (Prague 1954), 40–124.

[38] T. Slavova, 'Preslavska redakcija na Kirilo-Metodievija starobălgarski evangelski prevod', *Kirilo-Metodievski studii*, vi (1989), 15–129.

[39] On this feature in the Banica Gospel, see Lunt, op. cit. (n. 7), 68. See also Kossek, 'O leksike' (n. 30), 63, on a shared separate source for John in the Banica and Dobrejšo Gospels.

[40] E. Dogramadžieva, 'Ezikovo opisanie', in Dogramadžieva and Rajko, *Baniško evangelie*, (n. 5), 24–67, esp. 60–7. On the shortcomings of this lexical list, see Lunt, op. cit. (n. 7), 68.

with the Dobrejšo Gospel, but not consistently with the Zographensis, Marianus, or Tsar Ivan Alexander tetraevangelia. Where available, lexical variants from the Assemanianus, Koxno, and Plovdiv lectionaries are also given. The headwords are standardized: nouns and adjectives are given in the nominative singular, verbs in the infinitive.

Table 1

багрѣница: John 19: 5 (Zo, Mar, Ass **прапраждьна риза**; Dbrm, IvAl **багрѣна риза**); cf. John 19: 2 (**багрѣна риза**, also Dbrm, IvAl **риза багрѣна**; Dobrš **багрѣница**; Zo, Mar, Ass **риза прѣпраждьна**), Mark 15: 17 (Cur **прѣпражда**, Ban **опрѣпражда**, Zo **прапражда**, Mar **прапраждъ**, Ass **прѣпраждь**; folio missing from Dobrš), 15: 20 (Ban, Cur **прапражда**; Zo, Mar **прапраждъ**; Dbrm **багрѣница**; folio missing from Dobrš).

без оума: Mark 7: 7 (Zo, Mar, Dbrm, IvAl **въ соуе**; folio missing from Dobrš), John 15: 25 (also IvAl; Zo, Mar, Ass, Dbrm, Kox **спъıть**).

ближьнъ: Luke 10: 27 (Mar, Dbrm, Ass, IvAl, Kox, Plov **искрьнь**; Zo **подроугъ**); cf. Luke 10: 29, 10: 36 (**искрьнь**).

виноградъ: John 15: 1 (also Dbrm, IvAl; Zo, Mar, Ass, Kox, Plov **лоза**), 15: 4 (also Dbrm; Zo, Mar, Ass, IvAl, Plov **лоза**; phrase omitted from Kox), 15: 5 **виноградъ истинъıи** (Dbrm, IvAl **виноградъ ø**; Zo, Mar, Ass, Kox, Plov **лоза**).

водоточие: John 18: 1 (Mar, Ass, Dbrm, IvAl, Kox **потокъ**; Zo **островъ**).

вратарица: John 18: 16, 18: 17 (Zo, Ass, Dbrm, IvAl **двьрьница**; folio missing from Mar); cf. John 10: 3 (**двєрьникъ**).

градъ: John 18: 26 (Zo, Ass, Dbrm **вратъ**; IvAl **вратоградъ**; folio missing from Mar); John 19: 41 (Zo, Mar, Kox **вратъпъ**; Ass, Dbrm **вратъ**; IvAl **вратоградъ**); cf. expected **вратоградъ** in Luke 13: 19, and in Ban John 18: 1 (also IvAl, Kox; Dobrš **градъ**; Zo, Mar, Ass, Dbrm **вратъ**; phrase omitted from Cur).

долоу: Luke 4: 9 (Mar, Dbrm, IvAl, Kox **низъ**; folio missing from Zo), John 8: 6 (Zo, Mar, Dbrm, Kox **низъ**; this word is omitted from IvAl).

дѣлѣ/дѣли: John 12: 5 (Zo, Mar, Ass, Dbrm, IvAl, Plov **ради**; folio missing from Ban); cf. Luke 1: 78 and numerous occurrences of **ради** throughout.

жидове/жидовьскъ (Zo, Mar, Ass, Dbrm, IvAl, Kox, Plov **июдеи, июдеискъ**): John 12: 9 (folio missing from Ban), 12: 11 (also IvAl), 13: 33, 18: 12 (also IvAl), 18: 14, 18: 20, 18: 31, 18: 35 (**жидовинъ**: also Zo, Mar, Ass, IvAl; cf. Dbrm **июдеи**), 18: 36, 18: 38 (also Dbrm), 19: 3 (also Dbrm), 19: 7 (also Dbrm), 19: 12 (also Zo, Dbrm; folio missing from Ban), 19: 14 (also

Dbrm; folio missing from Ban),19: 20 and 19: 21 (folio missing from Ban), 19: 31, 19: 38, 19: 40, 19: 42, 20: 19; cf., for example, Mark 1: 5, 7: 3, and 15: 2, 15: 9, 15: 12 (Dbrm **жидовьскъ**), 15: 18, 15: 26 (folios missing from Dobrš); Luke 1: 5 (Dbrm **жидовьскъ**), 7: 3 (folio missing from Dobrš), 23: 3, 23: 37, 23: 38; John 1: 19, 2: 13, 2: 18, 3: 1 (Dbrm **жидовьскъ**, folio missing from Dobrš), 4: 9 (**июдеꙗнинь**, **июдеи**; Zo, Mar, Ass, Dbrm, IvAl **июдеи**, **июдеи**), 4: 22, 5: 1, 5: 10, 5: 15, 5: 18, 6: 4, 7: 1, 7: 2, 7: 35, 8: 22, 8: 48, 8: 52, 8: 57, 9: 22 (Dbrm **жидове**), 11: 31, 11: 45; John 18: 33 and 18: 39 (Ban, Cur, Dbrm **жидовьскъ**; Dobrš **июдеискъ**).

жизнь: John 12: 25 (Zo, Mar, Ass, Dbrm, IvAl, Kox, Plov **животъ**), 12: 50 (also IvAl; Zo, Mar, Dbrm **животъ**), 17: 2 (Zo, Mar, Ass, Dbrm, IvAl **животъ**; folio missing from Ban); cf. Mark 10: 17 (folio missing from Dobrš), Luke 18: 18, John 6: 33.

котыга: John 19: 23 (Zo, Mar, Dbrm, IvAl **хитонъ**; folio missing from Ban); 19: 24 (Zo, Mar, IvAl **матизмъ**; Dbrm illegible, later changed to **матизмъ**; folio missing from Ban).

лоза/лозие: John 15: 2 **лоза** (also Dbrm; Zo, Mar **разга**; Ass, IvAl, Kox, Plov **розга**), 15: 4 **лоза** (also Dbrm, Plov; Zo, Mar, Ass, IvAl, Kox **розга**), 15: 5 **лозие** (also Dbrm, IvAl; Zo, Mar, Kox **раждие**; Ass **рождие**; Plov **рождение**), 15: 6 **лозие** (Dbrm, IvAl **лоза**; Zo, Mar, Ass, IvAl, Kox, Plov **розга**).

масло: Luke 7: 46 (also Zo, Dbrm; Mar, Ass, Kox, Plov **олѣи**, IvAl **елеи**; folio missing from Dobrš); 10: 34 (also Zo, IvAl; Mar, Ass, Dbrm, Kox, Plov **олѣи**); 16: 6 (Zo, Mar, Dbrm **олѣи**; IvAl **елеи**).

масть благовоньнаꙗ: John 12: 3 (twice; Zo, Mar **хризма**, **хризмьнъ**; Ass **мѵро**, **мѵрьнъ**; Dbrm **мѵро**, **мѵрьнъ**; IvAl **мѵро**, **масть благовоньнаꙗ**; Kox **мѵро**, **хризмьнъ**; Plov **миро**, **измирьнъ**; folio missing from Ban); John 12: 5 (Zo **хризма**; Mar, Ass, Dbrm, Kox, Plov **мѵро**; IvAl apparently **масть**, later erased and replaced with **мѵро**); cf. shared **мѵро** in Mark 14: 3 (Zo, Mar **хризма**; Dbrm **мѵро благовоньны масти**, **мѵро**; IvAl **мастьнъ**), 14: 4 (Zo, Mar **хризмьнъ**; Dbrm **помазание**, IvAl **мастьнъ**), 14: 5 (also Dbrm; Zo, Mar **хризма**, IvAl **масть**); Luke 7: 37, 7: 38 (folio missing from Dobrš), 7: 46 (IvAl **масть**; folio missing from Dobrš), 23: 56 (Dbrm **крижма**, IvAl **помазание**); John 11: 2 (folio missing from Ban).

нѣкыи (Zo, Mar, Ass, Dbrm, IvAl **етеръ/единъ**): John 11: 37, 11: 46; cf. **етеръ/единъ** in Mark and Luke, and in earlier chapters of John; an exception for the Banica Gospel is Luke 17: 12 (Ban **нѣкыи**; also IvAl).

послоушьствовати (Zo, Mar, Ass, Dbrm, IvAl, Kox, Plov **съвѣдѣтельствовати**): John 12: 17, 15: 26, 15: 27, 18: 23, 18: 37; cf. shared **съвѣдѣтельствовати** in Mark 10: 19 (IvAl **послоушьствовати**; folio missing from Dobrš), 15: 4 (folio missing from Dobrš), Luke 4: 22, 11: 48 (Dobrš **съвѣдѣтельство**), John 2: 25 (Dbrm **послоушьствовати**, IvAl **съвѣстити**), 3: 26 (Ass **послоушьствовати**), 3: 32 (Ass **послоушьствовати**), 5: 31, 5: 32, 5: 33, 5: 36, 5: 37, 7: 7 (IvAl **послоушьствовати**), 8: 13, 8: 14, 8: 18 (IvAl **послоушьствовати**; sentence omitted from Cur), 10: 25.

Table 2

Mar (Zo, Ass, Kox, Plov)	IvAl	Dbrm	Dobrš	Ban	Cur
Mark 1:21					
на соньмищи	вь сънмище	—	вь зборище	вь зборище	вь зборище
Mark 1:23					
на соньмихъ [*sic*]	вь сънмищинихъ [*sic*]	—	на зборищихь	на сьборищи	на сьборищи
Mark 1:29					
и-съньмишта	изь сънмища	—	изь сънмища	и-сьнмища	сьньмища
Mark 1:39					
на сънъмиштихъ	на сънмищихъ	—	на сборищихь	на сьборищихь	на сьборыщихь
Mark 3:1					
въ сньмиште	въ сънмище	вь соньмище	в зборище	вь сѫборище	вь с'борище
Mark 6:2					
на сьнмишти	на сьнмищи	на соньмищи	на сборищи	на сьборищи	на сьборищи
Mark 12:39					
на соньмиштихъ	на сьнмищихъ	на соньміщихь	на сьборищихь	на сьборищихь	на зборищихь
Mark 13:9					
въ сънѧтиѣ	въ съ⟨нѧтиꙗ⟩[41]	вь сьборища	—	вь сборища	вь зборища
на сънъмищихъ	на сьнмищихъ	вь сьборѣхь	—	на зборищихь	на сьборищи
Luke 4:15					
на сънъмищихъ	на сънмищихъ	на соньмищихь	на съборишихъ	на сьборищиˣ	на сьборищихь
Luke 4:16					
въ сънъмиште	въ сънмище	въ соньмище	въ сборище	вь сьборище	вь зборыще
Luke 4:28					
на съньмишти	на съборїщи	—	на съборищихь	вь сьборищихь	вь зборищихь

Luke 4:38					
и–съньмишта	из сьнмища	оть соньмища	изь зборища	и–сьборища	и–зборища
Luke 4:44					
на съньмиштихъ	на сьньмищихъ	на соньмищихь	на сборищихь	на сьборищихь	на сборищихь
Luke 6:6					
въ съньмиште	вь съньмище	вь сонмище	—	вь сьборище	вь сьборыще
Luke 7:5					
съньмиште	сьнмище	сьборище	—	сьборище	сьборище
Luke 8:41					
съньмиштю	съньмищоу	сьборищоу	сьборищоу	сьборищȣ	зборищоу
Luke 11:43					
на съньмиштихь	на сънмищихъ	на сьнмищихь	на зборищихь	на сьборищихь	на сьборищихь
Luke 12:11					
на соньмишта	на сьнмища	на соньмища	на сборища	на сьборища	на зборища
Luke 13:10					
отъ соньмишть	ѿ сънмищь	оть сн҃мищь	ѿ сънмищъ	ѿ сьнмищь	ѿ сьнмищь
John 6:59					
на сонъмищи	на съборищи	на соньмищи	на зборищи	на сьборищи	на сьборыщи
John 9:22					
ø соньмишта	ø събора	ø сьньмища	ø съборища	ѿ сьборища	ѿ сьборища
John 12:42					
и-съньмиштъ	из сьнмища	оть соньмищь	ѿ съборищъ	ѿ сьборища	ѿ сьборища
John 16:2					
отъ съньмиштъ	ѿ сьнъмищь	оть соньмищь	ѿ сьборищъ	ѿ сьборищь	ѿ сьборищь
John 18:20 (Missing from Mar)					
Zo: на сънъмишти	на сьборищихь	на сьборищихь	въ зборищихъ	вь сьборищихь	вь сьборищихь

старѣшина жьрьчьскъ (Zo, Mar, Ass, Dbrm, IvAl, Kox, Plov **архиереи**): John 11: 57 (Zo, Mar, Dbrm, IvAl **архиереи и фарисѣи**; folio missing from Ban), 12: 10 (Zo,Mar, Dbrm, Plov **архиереи**; IvAl **архиереи и книжници**), 18: 3 (Dbrm **стар(ѣ)и**, later changed to **старѣшина жьрьчьскъ**), 18: 10, 18: 13 (Dobrš **старѣишина ø**), 18: 15, 18: 16, 18: 19, 18: 22, 18: 24, 18: 35, 19: 6 (also Dbrm); cf. John 11: 47 (**архиереи и фарисѣи**; Dobrš **архиереи съ фарисеи**), and **архиереи** in Mark and Luke.

цѧта: Luke 12: 59 (Zo, Mar, Dbrm **тръхъть**; IvAl **коньдрать**), John 12: 5 (folio missing from Ban; Zo, Mar, Ass, Dbrm, IvAl, Kox **пѣнѧѕь**; Plov **сьребрьникъ**); cf. Luke 20: 24 (**златица**; Zo, Mar, Dbrm, IvAl **пѣнѧѕь**), and shared **пѣнѧѕь** in John 2: 15 (Ass **сьребро**), 6: 7.

ꙗгодичина: Luke 19: 4 (also IvAl, later erased; Zo, Mar, Ass, Dbrm, Plov **сѵкомориꙗ**; IvAl **сѵкомориꙗ**, later changed to **ꙗгодичина**; Plov **соухоморика**).

A particularly persuasive lexical indicator of a common ancestry with the Dobrejšo Gospel is the strict correspondence among the three manuscripts in the distribution of the variants **съньмище** and **съборище** in Mark, Luke, and John. In contrast to the Codex Zographensis, the Codex Marianus, and the lectionaries, all of which consistently use **съньмище**, the Dobrejšo, Banica, and Curzon Gospels use the variant **съборище** throughout Mark, Luke, and John, but, exceptionally, in Mark 1: 29 and Luke 13: 10, all three manuscripts have **съньмище**. The Dobromir and Tsar Ivan Alexander Gospels bridge the gap, as it were, by using **съньмище** predominantly, but with isolated occurrences of **съборище** (e.g. Dbrm in Mark 13: 9, Luke 7: 5, 8: 14, John 18: 20; IvAl in Luke 4: 28, John 6: 59, 9: 22 **събора**, 18: 20). Table 2 below offers an overview of the distribution of **съньмище** and **съборище** in the tetraevangelia. Their distribution in Matthew is discussed in section 4 below. Particularly telling are the coincidences between the Curzon, Banica, and Dobrejšo Gospels in the use of the preposition **на** versus **въ** with **съборище**.

[41] Apparently originally **сънѧтиꙗ**; changed to **сьвⷪрища** by a later hand.

The Curzon, Banica, and Dobrejšo versions of Mark, Luke, and John also share a number of syntactic correspondences. Particularly indicative of a common textual tradition with the Dobrejšo Gospel and, to some extent, the earlier Dobromir Gospel is the dative absolute **прѣклоньшоу же сѧ дн҃и** that begins Luke 9: 12. This phrase, which is also shared by the Dobromir Gospel, stands in contrast to the variant in the Zographensis, Marianus and Tsar Ivan Alexander tetraevangelia, namely **дьнь же начѧтъ прѣкланѣти сѧ**, which is closer to the standard Greek text (Ἡ δὲ ἡμέρα ἤρξατο κλίνειν).[42] The dative absolute is particularly interesting because, as indicated by the placement of the liturgical instruction in the Curzon, Banica, and Dobromir Gospels, it is not part of the lection that begins in the same verse (liturgical instructions are not shown by Conev in the printed edition of the Dobrejšo Gospel).[43]

Cur (fol. 95^{v}, ll. 13–15), Ban, Dobrš, Dbrm (**Дьни же прѣ|клоньшоу сѧ оуже**): **Прѣклоньшоу же сѧ дни.** {**в пѧ^к д҃ не^д ѿ лоу^к в о^н мѧ | за^ч**} **Пристѧпльше же ѡба на десѧте** <**же**> **рѣшѧ к|моу. Ѿпоусти народы.**

IvAl (fol. 164^{v}, ll. 15–20), Zo, Mar: {**к^ц чр^к**} **Дн҃ь же начѧтъ прѣкланѣти сѧ** {**за^ч**} **Пристѫ|стѫпльше** [*sic*] **же оба на десѧте, рекошѫ к|моу. Ѿпоусти народы.**

Another syntactic correspondence occurs in John 19: 31. Here the Curzon, Banica, and Dobrejšo Gospels share a distinctive positioning of the subordinate clause:

Cur (fol. 169^{r}, l. 23 – fol. 169^{v}, l. 1), Ban, Dobrš: **Жидове же вьпросишѧ пи|лата. да не ѡстанѧть тѣлеса на кр^стѣ| вь сѧ^бтѧ. вѣ бо великь дн҃ь тоѧ сѧботы. | мл҃ишѧ да прѣбиѧть голѣни ихь. и вьзма^т. || понеже пѧ^к вѣ.**

Mar, Zo, Ass, Dbrm (**понеже параскеу**{**г**}**иѣ| вѣ** positioned after **вь сѫботѫ**, later corrected to Zo Mar Ass version), IvAl (fol. 266^{v}, ll. 10–15, **понеже пѧтокъ вѣ/вѣше** appearing twice, in Zo Mar Ass position and in Dbrm position), Kox, Plov: **Іюдеи же понеже параскевь|ћи вѣ. да не останѫтъ нѣ̑стѣ тѣлеса. | въ соботѫ. вѣ бо великъ день тоѭ со|ботъı. молишѧ пилата да прѣбиѭ|тъ голѣни ихъ. і възъмѫтъ ѩ.**

Οἱ οὖν Ἰουδαῖοι, ἐπεὶ παρασκευὴ ἦν, ἵνα μὴ μείνῃ ἐπὶ τοῦ σταυροῦ τὰ σώματα ἐν τῷ σαββάτῳ, ἦν γὰρ μεγάλη ἡ ἡμέρα ἐκείνου τοῦ

[42] All Greek citations are from E. Nestle *et al.* (eds.), *Novum Testamentum Graece*, 26 ed. (Stuttgart, 1979).

[43] I am indebted to Horace G. Lunt for bringing this item to my attention.

σαββάτου, ἠρώτησαν τὸν Πιλᾶτον ἵνα κατεαγῶσιν αὐτῶν τὰ σκέλη καὶ ἀρθῶσιν.

The Curzon and Dobrejšo Gospels also share the occurrences of the construction **аще** Ø[...] **то** noted in Dogramadžieva's discussion of syntactic idiosyncrasies of the Banica Gospel (cf. Zo, Mar, Ass, Dbrm, IvAl, Kox, Plov **аще** Ø):[44] see Mark 7: 3, 9: 23, Luke 13: 9, 14: 32, 19: 31 (text missing from Dobrš), John 15: 20, 18: 36; cf. Cur **аще** Ø, Ban/Dobrš **аще** [...] **то** in John 8: 42, and numerous parallel occurrences of **аще** Ø, including Luke 11: 18, 13: 5; John 9: 22, etc.

A number of textual omissions from the Banica and Curzon Gospels also occur in the Dobrejšo Gospel. One example is John 10: 11, where these three tetraevangelia follow the tradition of the lectionary gospels by containing only one instance of the phrase **пастырь добры**. However, while the Banica and Curzon Gospels also follow the lectionaries in using a first-person singular verb (changed in the latter to **полагаѧ**^{т} by corrector A), the Dobrejšo version agrees with the other tetraevangelia in having a third-person verb:

Cur (fol. 151^{r},ll. 6–7), Ban: **азь ѥсьмь пастирь до|бри.** <...>**дш҇ѧ своѧ полагаѧ за ѡвцѧ.**

Dobrš: **азъ есъмъ пастырь ѡвцамъ добры.** <...> **дш҇ѫ своѫ полагаеть за ѡвцѧ.**

Dbrm, Zo, Mar, IvAl: **азь | есмь пастырь добръı: пастырь добрыї | доушѫ своѭ полагаеть за овьцѧ: |**

Ass, Kox, Plov: **Азь ес|мъ пастъирь до|бръи.** <...> **И дш҇ѫ сво|ѭ полагаѭ | за овцѧ.**

Ἐγώ εἰμι ὁ ποιμὴν ὁ καλός. ὁ ποιμὴν ὁ καλὸς τὴν ψυχὴν αὐτοῦ τίθησιν ὑπὲρ τῶν προβάτων.

Another example of a shared omission is to be found in Luke 4: 37:

Cur (fol. 84^{v}, l. 16), Ban, Dobrš: **исхож**^{д}**аше** <...> **вьсѧ мѣсто и страни.**

Dbrm, Zo, Mar, IvAl: **И исхождааше шоумь о немь. | во вьсѣко мѣсто. и страны.**

καὶ ἐξεπορεύετο ἦχος [or: ἐξῆλθεν ἡ ἀκοὴ] περὶ αὐτοῦ εἰς πάντα τόπον τῆς περιχώρου.

John 4: 24 presents two points of interest: a shared omission and independent anomalies in the Curzon and Dobrejšo Gospels. Here

[44] Dogramadžieva, 'Ezikovo opisanie', in Dogramadžieva and Rajkov, *Baniško evangelie* (n. 5), 60.

the Curzon Gospel version contains a repetition as well as the shared omission, while the Dobrejšo Gospel's omission is more extensive than that of the other two manuscripts. The Codex Zographensis preserves verse 24 intact, but it too contains an omission in the vicinity, losing verse 22 and the first half of verse 23.

Cur (fol. 136^{v}, ll. 18–23): 23 [...] ѥг^{д}а истини поклоници поклонѧть сѧ.| дх҇омь истыноѧ. ѡц҃ь бо тацѣхь ище|ть. кланѣѧщих сѧ ѥмоу дх҇омь исти|ноѧ. ѡц҃ь бо тацѣхь ищеть. кланѣѧщи|хь сѧ ѥмоу 24 <...>дх҇омь истиноѧ. <и> достоі|ить кланѣти сѧ. [45]

Ban: 23 [...] ѥг^{д}а истиньнии покло|ницы поклонѫт сѧ. дх҇омь истинож. и оц҃ь | бо тацѣхь ищеть. кланѣжщих сѧ ѥмоу. | 24 <...> дх҇омь истинож. достоить кланѣти сѧ.

Dobrš: 23 [..] егда истинънии поклоници поклонѫт сѧ дх҇омь и истинож. <...> 24 <...> достоитъ кланѣти сѧ.

Mar, Zo (starting after отц҃ю), Ass, Dbrm, IvAl, Kox (verse 24 only): 23 [..] егда истиньни по|клоньници поклонѧтъ сѧ | отц҃ю. дх҇омь и истиноѭ. ібо отц҃ъ та|цѣхъ иштетъ покланѣѭштихъ сѧ емоу. | 24 дх҇ъ естъ б҃ъ. і иже кланѣатъ сѧ емоу | дх҇мь и истиноѭ достоитъ кланѣти сѧ. |

καὶ γὰρ ὁ πατὴρ τοιούτους ζητεῖ τοὺς προσκυνοῦντας αὐτόν. πνεῦμα ὁ θεός, καὶ τοὺς προσκυνοῦντας αὐτὸν ἐν πνεύματι καὶ ἀληθείᾳ δεῖ προσκυνεῖν.

An omission in John 6: 33 is also shared with the Dobromir Gospel:

Cur (fol. 141^{v}, ll. 22–4, Ban, Dobrš, Dbrm (missing phrase added later in margin): 32 [...] нь ѡц҃ь | мои. даѥть вамь хлѣбь истины сь | небесе. 33 <...> даѧ животь мироу. [46]

Mar, Zo, Ass, IvAl: 32 [...] нъ отц҃ъ мои да|стъ вамъ хлѣбъ истинъны съ небе|се. 33 хлѣбъ бо б҃жии естъ съходѧи с н҃бсе. | и даѩи живота мироу.

A significant number of the lexical, syntactic, and textual parallels between the Banica and Curzon Gospel versions of Mark, Luke, and John are not shared either with the Dobrejšo Gospel or consistently with any of the other manuscripts used in this article for comparative purposes. These parallels are persuasive evidence that these books in the Curzon and Banica Gospels were copied either from a single third manuscript, or, more likely, from two

[45] A superscript т has been added to the second ѡц҃ь (ѡ^{т}ць) by corrector A, who has also made corrections of ѧ to ж, resulting in поклонжть сѧ, истынож, and кланѣжщих сѧ/ кланѣжщихь сѧ.

[46] Corrector A has added a superscript т to ѡц҃ь (ѡ^{т}ць), has corrected the ѧ in даѧ to ж, and has added a superscript и immediately thereafter (даж^{и}).

very closely related manuscripts. Lexical items shared solely with the Banica Gospel include the following four which (with the exception of ѡвоуши) are in Dogramadžieva's list of lexical idiosyncrasies of the Banica Gospel.

връзовль: Luke 16: 7 (Dobrš, IvAl мѣръ; Dbrm кринь; Zo коръ, Mar, корецъ).

ѡвоуши: Mark 1: 7 (Dobrš сапогь; Zo, Ass, IvAl сапогоу; Mar чрѣвиемъ, folio missing from Dbrm).

ѡврѧчницеѧ: Luke 2: 5 (Ban ѡврѫчницеѫ; Dbrš, Zo, Mar, Ass, Dbrm, IvAl, Kox ѡврѫченоѫ).

оутѣшнѣють: Luke 8: 45 (Dobrš, Dbrm, Plov оугнѣтаеть; Zo, Mar оутѣштаѭть; Ass оутіскаѭтъ, IvAl оутѣскаѫть).

The distribution of съньмище and съборище presented in Table 2 above, pointing to a common source for the Banica and Curzon versions of Mark, is supplemented by further evidence involving these words. While the parallel addition of the preposition ѿ in John 9: 22 may have been independently inspired (Ban, Cur ѿлѧчень ѿ сьборища; cf. Dobrš Ø съборища, Zo, Mar, Ass, Dbrm, IvAl Ø сънъмишта), there is a more persuasive divergence from the Dobrejšo version in Luke 20: 46, where both the Curzon and the Banica Gospels have ѡбѣдѣхь, while omitting сьборище/зборище. There is an apparent connection between the omission and the shared lexical anomaly прѣжᵈесѣданиꙗ, which also appears in the Dobrejšo version, though in a different position:

Cur (fol. 120ᵛ, l. 20–1), Ban: прѣжᵈесѣда|ниꙗ [*sic*] <...> на ѡбѣдѣхь

Dobrš: прѣдъсѣдания на зборищихъ и прѣждесѣдания [*sic*] на ѡбѣдѣхъ

Mar, Zo, Ass (прѣдьзьваніѣ), Dbrm, IvAl (съборищихъ), Plov: прѣдъ|сѣдание на съньмихъ. [*sic*] и прѣждезъ|ваниѣ на обѣдѣхъ

A particularly interesting example of lexical coincidence between the Curzon and Banica Gospels is the verb призва in the opening liturgical rubric to Luke 9: 1, which appears in the actual text in both manuscripts as сьзва/сьзвавь; (also Zo, Mar, Ass съзъвавъ; cf. Dobrš, Plov призва; Dbrm, IvAl призьвавь):[47]

Cur (fol. 95ʳ, ll. 11–12): {сѫᴮ з̄ ѿ лоуᴷ. в оᴴмѧ при зaᶣ} | 1 Сьзва же ісᶜь ѡба на десѧте апᶜла.

[47] While the choice between participles and finite preterite verb forms in Bulgarian Church Slavonic manuscripts is often arbitrary, the distinction between the Curzon Gospel and the Banica Gospel in this particular instance may be of significance with respect to their individual origins, since the aorist сьзва in the Curzon version would be expected for the beginning of a lection, whereas the Banica Gospel's participle сьзвавь would be expected in the continuous text of a tetraevangelion.

Ban: {**Сж^Б .з̄. ѿ лоу^К. Б ѡ^Н врѣ^М. призва ісь за^Ч.**} 1 **Сьзвав' же** {**.не^Д.**} | **ісь оба на десѧте ап^Сла.**

An odd feature of the Curzon Gospel version of this lection that may be of some significance is the superscript **ош** in the verb **ид^ош ѧ** which appears in Luke 9: 11. It would be unusual to use superscript vowel and consonant letters together in this way, so this is more likely to be a correction of the third-person plural archaic aorist form **идѧ** (for OCS **идѫ**) to **идошѧ** (cf. Ban **идошѫ**). Although archaic aorists are infrequent in the Curzon Gospel, they are less so in the Banica Gospel.[48] Thus, if the superscript letters are indeed a correction, this suggests that archaic aorists may have appeared in the shared protograph and were replaced routinely in the Curzon Gospel, but only sporadically in the Banica Gospel.

The most striking lexical features shared by the two manuscripts include three isolated Graecisms. The presence of Graecisms in the Banica Gospel has been pointed out by Lunt as evidence of strong Greek influence.[49] One of them (in Matthew) is unique to the Banica Gospel (**камьмелоу** instead of Slavonic **вельбѫдоу**, Matt. 19: 24), but the other three occur in the same locations in the Curzon Gospel.[50] These are:

(i) the translation into Church Slavonic of the Greek place-name Decapolis in Mark 7: 31 as **десѧти гра^Д** (Cur **десѧти гради**, also Dobrš; cf. Zo **декапельскъı**; Mar, Ass, Dbrm, IvAl, Kox **декапольскъı**);

(ii) the Cyrillicization of Greek πιττάκιον as **питакь** in Luke 16: 6 (cf. Dobrš **книгъı**; Zo, Mar, Dbrm, IvAl **боукъви**);

(iii) two instances of the Cyrillicization of Greek σεισμός in the menology: Ban genitive **сисизма** [*sic*] (7 October; cf. Cur fol. 174^v, l. 25 **сизма**), and Ban dative **сисмȣ** (26 October, also Cur fol. 175^v, l. 7 **сисмоу**).

Of particular interest is the Graecism **алекторь/алехторь** (ἀλέκτωρ), which appears only in the Curzon Gospel in Mark. The corresponding passages in the Banica version of Mark have the

[48] See H. Lunt, op. cit. (n. 7), 66–7.

[49] Ibid. 68–9.

[50] Lunt (ibid. 68, 67) also comments on a Greek phrase in the note written by the scribe at the end of John and on several archaisms and post-OCS lexical innovations in the Banica Gospel. The forms mentioned by Lunt that appear in books other than Matthew are **трьжще** (for OCS **тьржще**, Mark 7: 3; the Curzon variant is **трѧще**, changed by corrector A to **трищи**), **отрь** (Luke 7: 44, also Cur), and the aorist form **вдаде** (Luke 19: 23; Cur **да**); cf. **рѣснотѫ** (Matt. 26: 73, Cur **истынѧ**).

word **кокоть**. In Matthew, Luke, and John, however, the Banica Gospel uses a different word, **пѧтель**, where the Curzon Gospel shares with the Dobrejšo Gospel the peculiar nominative singular form **коурѧ** (Luke 22: 34, 60, 61; John 13: 38, 18: 27; see also discussion of Matthew in section 4 below). The fact that in Mark both the Curzon and the Banica Gospels have variants other than the usual **пѧтель** or **коурѧ** suggests that in Mark the protograph too had some other word (cf. Mark 13: 35: Cur, Dobrš, Zo, Dbrm, IvAl **кꙋрѧглашениѥ** (IvAl changed to **петлоглашение**), Ban **пѧтлоглашениѥ**, Mar **кокотоглашение**). Although all the verses from Mark referring to the cock crowing are now missing from the Dobrejšo Gospel, the distribution of lexical variants follows the same general pattern as the variants presented in Tables 1 and 2 above.

Zo	Mar	IvAl	Dbrm	Dobrš	Ban	Cur
Mark 14: 30						
коуръ	**кокотъ**	**пѧтелъ**	**пѧтела**	—	**кокоть**	**алехторь**[51]
Mark 14: 68						
коуръ	**кокотъ**	**пѧтель**	**пѧтель**	—	**кокоть**	**алекторь**
Mark 14: 72						
коуръ	**кокотъ**	**пѧтелъ**[52]	**пѧтель**	—	**кокоть**	**алекторь**
коуръ	**кокотъ**	**пѧтелъ**	**пѧтель**	—	**кокоть**	**алехторь**

On the syntactic level, the Banica and Curzon Gospels share certain anomalies which suggest defects in the protograph. One example is the nominative reflexive possessive adjective **своꙗ** for expected **моꙗ** in John 10:14:

Cur (fol. 151^{r}, l. 14), Ban (**зна|ѫть мѧ**): **Азь ѥсьмь пастирь добри. и азь знаѧ| моѧ и знаѥть мѧ своа**;[53] cf. Dobrš **мои** ; Zo, Mar, Ass, Dbrm, IvAl **моѩ**; Kox **моа**, Plov **знаѧт мѧ ѡвци имѧ мое**).[54]

Other distortions shared by the two manuscripts include the following:

[51] Corrected from **алекторь**, apparently by the original primary scribe.

[52] Apparently originally **пѧтелъ** in both instances, the **е** being erased and changed to **ь** by a later hand.

[53] A superscript **и** has been added to **добри (добри^и^)** by corrector A, who has also corrected **знаѧ** to **знаѫ** and **моѧ** to **моа**.

[54] Conev, 'Knižovni starini' (n. 5), 25, notes that the reflexive form **свои** in the Banica Gospel also occurs once in the nominative in place of a non-reflexive form in Mark 14: 12 (**гл҃ашѫ ѥмꙋ оученицы свои**) and twice with a dative antecedent: Matt. 25: 15 (**И ѡвомꙋ да^с^ .е҃. та|ланьѳь. ѡвомꙋ .в҃. ѡвомꙋ .а҃. комꙋ|жд^о^ противѫ своѥи. силѣ**) and Mark 13: 1 (where the antecedent appears as the indirect object and in a dative absolute: **Исходѧщꙋ ѥмꙋ ѿ цр҃кве. гл҃а ѥмꙋ ѥдин|нь ѿ оученикь своихь**). Conev treats these occurrences as innovations, but all three anomalies occur not only in the Curzon Gospel (including the verse from Matthew, which is a different redaction), but also in the Dobrejšo Gospel and in Zographensis and Marianus.

(i) use of a neuter plural noun (or perhaps, in the Curzon version, feminine singular for neuter plural) in Luke 8: 5: Cur **ѡва паде**, Ban **ова падѫ**; cf. Zo, Mar, Ass, Dbrm, IvAl, Plov neuter singular **ово паде** (folio missing from Dobrš);

(ii) Ban **хотѧть**, Cur **хотѣть**[55] for **ходѧтъ** in Mark 7: 5; cf. Zo, Mar, IvAl **ходѧтъ**, Dbrm **походѧть**, later corrected to **ходѧть** (folio missing from Dobrš);

(iii) Cur, Ban **приде ѿ гали|леѩ** for **приде отъ июдеѩ въ галилеѭ** in John 4: 47; cf. Dobrš, Zo, Mar, Ass, Dbrm, IvAl (ἥκει ἐκ τῆς Ἰουδαίας εἰς τὴν Γαλιλαίαν).

A further example of shared garbling occurs in John 2: 11, where both the Banica and the Curzon versions appear to reflect a defect in the protograph:

Cur (fol. 133r,ll. 17–18): **се створы нѧчѧтькь<і>**[56]**зна** <--->| **ісⷭь.**
Ban: **се створи начѧткы знаѥмы іс҃ь.**
Dobrš **се твори** <...> **знамениемъ ис҃ъ**
Dbrm: **Се же створи зачѧтокь знаме|мениемь**[*sic*] **їс҃сь.**
IvAl (fol.217r, ll. 19–20), Zo, Mar, Ass: **се сътвори начѧ|токъ знамениемь іс҃**

Here the Banica Gospel uses **знаѥмы** for **знамениемъ**. The equivalent word in the Curzon Gospel has been partially erased, and the erased portion, which consisted of three, or possibly four, letters after the fragment **зна**, has been replaced by corrector A with the letters **мении**. Although the erased letters cannot be deciphered with certainty, the amount of space taken up by the erasure is consistent with the amount of space required for the letters **ѥмы** in the primary hand. That both manuscripts contain a garbling and truncation of the same word to roughly the same length suggests either that both the Curzon and Banica scribes may have been reproducing the form **знаѥмы** directly from the protograph or that they may have been making independent attempts to reconstruct a word that was garbled or illegible in the protograph. There may be some connection between the origin of this shared truncation and another sort of garbling of the same word in the Dobromir Gospel, i.e. dittography at line-end consisting of repetition of a syllable in the distorted form **знаме|мениемь**. The Dobrejšo Gospel, however, contains the word **знамениемъ** intact. Further evidence of a shared source for this passage is the unusual plural form **нѧчѧтькы**, which appears only in the Banica and Curzon versions (and is omitted

[55] Corrected to **хотѧть** by corrector B.
[56] The form **нѧчѧтькы** has been corrected to **нѧчѧтькь** by corrector A.

altogether from the passage in the Dobrejšo Gospel).[57] The Curzon Gospel also contains a pronoun substitution in Luke 11: 23 which has a counterpart in the Banica Gospel:[58]

Cur (fol. 101ʳ, ll. 23–4), Ban: **Иже нѣсть сь мноѧ на | вы ѥсть.**

Dobrš, Zo, Mar, Dbrm, IvAl: **Иже нѣсть съ мноѫ на мѧ есть.**

῾Ο μὴ ὢν μετ᾽ ἐμοῦ κατ᾽ ἐμοῦ ἐστιν

The Curzon and Banica versions of Mark, Luke, and John also contain a number of identical distortions and omissions. The number and character of these parallel features, some of which are illustrated in the excerpts below, suggest that they are innovations introduced in a common ancestor. One such correspondence concerns the Banica Gospel's Cyrillicized Greek headings to Luke and John.[59] While both manuscripts have similar Slavonic headings for Mark (Cur fol. 44ʳ, l.13, Ban plate, fol. 61ʳ), a Greek heading for Luke appears in the Banica Gospel alone. The Curzon Gospel does, however, contain a Cyrillicized Greek heading for John that is nearly identical in form with the Banica Gospel's: indeed, here both manuscripts have nom.-acc. **то** for the expected Cyrillicized Greek genitive form **тоү** in the phrase **ѥк то ката їωннынь** (ἐκ τοῦ κατὰ ᾽Ιωάννην); this shared distortion suggests a defect or ambiguity in the shared source. The Banica heading sandwiches the name **їωнь** between the two portions of the Cyrillicized Greek word **ката**:

Cur (fol. 130ᵛ, l. 6): **ѥѵᴳлиѥ ѿ иѡᴴ ѥк то катѧ | иωᴴнынь на паскѧ глаᴮ а҃**

Ban (plate, fol, 148ʳ): **ѥѵᴳлиѡᴴ. |ѥк то кѧ|. їѡнь. | тѧ иѡнинь. ѥѵᴳлїѥ иѧ пᶜсѫ**

The Banica Gospel also shares the wording and mid-verse location of the Curzon Gospel's large heading immediately preceding John 13: 31, and a homoeoteleuton in verse 32 which occurs also in the Koxno lectionary:

[57] Another example of garbling that is shared with the Dobromir Gospel is the occurrence of a clause in Luke 6:18 containing a reflexive verb together with a participle in the genitive or genitive-accusative rather than the nominative (Cur **стражᴬащихь**, Ban **стражᴬѫщᴵхь**; see discussion of Cur **а–ѧ** confusion in section 2 above): Cur (fol. 88ʳ, ll. 5–6), Ban, Dbrm (fol. missing from Dobrš): **и стражᴬащихь ѿ дх҃ь нечтихь. |исцѣлѧхᶜѧ.** Cf. Zo, Mar, IvAl, Ass, Kox, Plov: **стражд҄ѫ|штеі. отъ дх҃ъ нечистъ. | цѣлѣахѫ сѧ.** (οἱ ἐνοχλούμενοι ἀπὸ πνευμάτων ἀκαθάρτων ἐθεραπεύοντο).

[58] Observed by Lunt, op. cit. (n. 7), 68.

[59] See discussion ibid. Facsimiles of the Banica headings appear as plates in Dogramadžieva and Rajkov, *Baniško evangelie* (n. 5), unnumbered pages.

Cur (fol. 159r, ll. 19–24), Ban (without за^{ч}, and additionally with expected ѩече же іс҃ь in text, immediately before нн҃ѣ): 31 ѥг^{д}а изыде | {ѤѸ^{г}Є Ӑ НА СТР^{С}ТЬ іѠ^{Н}: за^{ч} | ѩе^{ч} г҃ь своимь ѹченикомь} <...> Нн҃ѣ просла|вьї сѧ сн҃ь члвч^{с}кы. и б҃ь прославы | сѧ ѡ немь. 32 <...> и б҃ь прославыты ѡ себѣ. | авыѥ прославыты и.[60]

Kox (without егда же изъıде): ЄѴА^{Г}ЛІА ЕІ НА СТР^{С}ТИ ГЛЕЪ:.}| 31<...> Ре^{ч} г҃ъ своимъ оученикомь. нн҃ѣ | прослави сѧ сн҃ъ члвчк^{с}ы. и б҃ъ про|слави сѧ о немь. 32 <...> и б҃ъ прослави|тыи въ себѣ. авие прославѧть и ||

Dobrš (also Zo, Mar, Dbrm, Ass (without егда же изъıде and with Рече г҃ь кь с|воимъ оу|ченіком for Ре^{ч} же ис҃ъ), IvAl): 31 егда же изъıде: Ре^{ч} же ис҃ъ. нынѣ прослави сѧ сн҃ъ чл вч҃ьскыи и б҃ъ прослави сѧ ѡ немъ. 32 аще б҃ъ прославит сѧ ѡ немь. и б҃ъ прославитъї-и въ себѣ: авие прославить ї.

Two identical errors caused by homoeoteleuta occur in John 3: 29–30, including the perseverative радость for расти in John 3: 30, which appears in both the Banica and Dobrejšo Gospels and seems to have been shared originally by the Curzon Gospel as well: the two letters о^{с} in the fragment рад<о^{с}> have been erased and replaced with сти by corrector A (cf. Mar, Ass, Dbrm, IvAl расти; (ἐκεῖνον δεῖ αὐξάνειν; folio missing from Zo).

Cur (fol. 135r, l.26–fol. 135v, l. 7), Ban:

29 Имѣѧ невѣстѧ женихь ѥсть. ||
а дроугь жениховь. си бо
радо^{с} моѩ и|спльни сѧ. да
ѡномоу подобаѥть радо^{с}. | а
мнѣ мнить сѧ. а дроугь
жениховь | стоѧ и послоушаѧ
ѥго. ра^{д}<у>стиѧ ра^{д}уѥ|ть сѧ.
за гла^{с} жениховь. си бо радость |
моѩ испльни сѧ. 30 да ѡномоу
п^{д}обаѥть. | рад<о^{с}>. а мнѣ мнить
сѧ.[61]

Dobrš (also Mar, Ass, Dbrm, IvAl):

29 Имѣѫи невѣстѫ женихъ есть.
а дроугь жениховь стоѫ и
послоушаѫ его радостиѫ
радоует сѧ за гласъ жениховъ.
си бо радость моꙗ испл҄ни сѧ.
30 да ѡномоу подобаеть
радость. а мнѣ мнит сѧ.

[60] Corrector A has added the word ѥго in the margin after the first прославыты, has changed the point after члвч^{с}кь to a comma, and has inserted the conjunction и immediately before авыѥ.

[61] Alterations here (all apparently by corrector A) are the addition of a superscript и after Имѣѧ in the first line (Имѣѧ^{и}), the addition of a superscript и after стоѧи (стоѧи ^{и}), the alteration of послоушаѧ to послоушаѫ, the addition of superscript ь and ї to мнить сѧ (м^{ь}нить^{ї} сѧ), and the alteration of the second моѩ to моꙗ. It appears that the primary scribe at first began to write the word раѹ^{д}стиѧ (with аѹ ligature) as раѹ^{д}ет сѧ in anticipation of the phrase that immediately follows, but, having written the fragment раѹ^{д}, caught the error in mid word, added the letter с instead of є, and erased the ѹ, forming ра^{д}стиѧ. The corrector further altered the word to ра^{д}о^{с}тиѫ, which is closer to the primary scribe's abbreviations of this word earlier in the passage. The corrector has also struck out the repetition and has added the following version of the text in the top margin: стоєи и слишаѫ ѥго, радо^{с}ти радѹе^{т} се.

Each manuscript also exhibits two homoeoteleuta within the space of seven verses, through omission of Luke 19: 18–19 and 19: 25:

Luke 19: 17–20, 24–6

Cur (fol. 117ʳ, ll. 23–5), Ban	Dobrš (also Zo, Mar, Ass, Dbrm, IvAl, all with ѿимать)
17 [...] бѧди ѡбласть ими на десѧти гради. ǀ <...> 20 И дроугы приде гл҃ѧ ги҃ се манаⷭ твои[62] ꙗже ǀ имахь положень вь оуброусѣ. [...]	17 [...] бѫди область имꙑи надъ десѧтиѭ градꙑ. 18 и приде вторыи гл҃ѫ. манасъ твоꙗ гⷣи сътвори .є҃. манасъ. 19 реⷱ же и томоу и тꙑ бѫди натъ [*sic*] .є҃. градь. 20 И дроугы приде гл҃ѫ. гⷣи се манасъ твоꙗ ѭже имѣхъ положенъ въ оброусѣ [*sic*] [...]
(fol. 117ᵛ, ll. 10-13)	
24 [...] и дадите имѧшомоу.г҃. маǀнась. <...> 26 и реⷱ. Ꙗмн҃ь гл҃ѧ вамь. ꙗко вьсѣǀкомоу имѧшомоу даⷭ сѧ. а ѿ не имѧǀшаго. иже имать ѿимать ѿ него.ǀ	24 [...] дадите имѫщомоу .г҃. манасъ. 25 рѣшѫ емоу. гⷣі. имать .г҃. манасъ. 26 и реⷱ: Ꙗминъ гл҃ѫ вамъ. ꙗко всѣкомоу имѫщомоу дастъ сѧ. а ѿ не имѫщаго и еже имать <...> ѿ него.

The parallel omission of the sentence **ни сѫдите, да не сѫдѧтъ вамъ** in the excerpt below is of particular interest because this phrase appears in an unusual location in the earlier Dobromir Gospel, immediately after the similar sentence **и не осѫждаите да не осѫдѧть вась**, rather than before it, as expected. This suggests that the omission arose as the result of a scribe's encounter with a Dobromir-type inversion of the text at some point in the common ancestry. Unfortunately, the passage is now missing from the Dobrejšo Gospel.

Luke 6: 36–7

Cur (fol. 88ᵛ, l. 26 –fol. 89ʳ, l. 2), Ban: 36 **бѧⷣте млрⷣи ꙗко ѡц҃ь вашь**

[62] Cf. OCS **мънасъ** (indeclinable) or **мънаса** (Gr. μνᾶ), both feminine. The masculine variant **манась/манасъ** appears consistently throughout this passage in the Curzon and Dobromir Gospels; the Banica version also has **манась** in verses 16 and 20, but treats it as feminine (**манась твоꙗ**). While the Dobrejšo version also uses the feminine possessive adjective with **манась**, the accusative past passive participle **положень**, occurring with it in verse 20 of both the Curzon and the Dobrejšo Gospels, is masculine; cf. Ban **положенѫ**.

млсрдь нс. || {коц нед в вркь. г. нед ѿ лоук реч гл} 37<...> Не ωсаждаите да | не ωсѧдѧть вась.

Dbrm: 36 Бѫдѣ|те оубо милосрьди. ꙗкоже и оц҃ь вашь милосрдь ѥсть. | {.коц.} 37 И не осѫждаите да не осѫдѧть | вась. ни сѫдите да не сѫдѧть вамь.

Mar, Zo, IvAl: 36 бѫдѣте оубо ми|лостиви. ꙗкоже и отецъ вашъ мило|срдъ естъ {.·.кц.·.} 37 і не сѫдите да не | сѫдѧтъ вамъ. не осѫждаите да | не осѫдѧтъ васъ.

Similar parallel omissions can be found in Mark and John:

Mark 2: 18–19

Cur (fol. 47r, ll. 4–7), Ban (also фарисеисти): 18 [...] по что оученици | иωнви и фарисеисти постѣть сѧ. <...> 19 и реч и|мь іс҃ь. ѥда могѧть снове брачни пости|ти сѧ.

Dobrš (also Zo, Mar, Dbrm, IvAl, all with твои оученици): 18 [...] по что оученици иωанови и фарисеи постѧт сѧ. а твои <...> не постѧт сѧ. 19 реч имъ исъ еда могѫть снве брачнии постити сѧ.

Mark 4: 13

Cur (fol. 49v, l. 10), Ban: и гл҃а имь <...> притчѣ сеѧ.
Dobrš (also Zo, Mar, Dbrm, IvAl): и гл҃а имь. не вѣсте ли причѧ сиѧ.

Mark 5: 40–1

Cur (fol. 52v, ll. 3–6), Ban: 40 и рѧга|хѧ сѧ ѥмоу. ωнь же изгна всѧ. <...> и поѧть ωт҃ца ωтроковыцѧ. <...> 41 и гл҃а ѥи. талиѳакоу|мь.

Dobrš (also Zo, Mar, Dbrm, IvAl; the garbled word воѧнъ and its later correction to вънъ are unique to the Dobrejšo version; cf. Gr. ἐκβαλὼν πάντας): 40 и рѫгаіахѫ сѧ емоу. ωн же изгна всѧ воѧнъ [*sic*] поѧть ωц҃а и[*sic*] ѿтроковицѧ и матере. и иже бѣшѫ с нимъ. и вниде идеже бѣ ѿрочѧ лежѫ. 41 и емь за рѫкѫ ѿроковицѫ и гл҃а еи: талиѳакоумь.

Mark 9: 50

Cur (fol. 61r, l. 17), Ban: [...] имѣите соль вь себѣ. <...>

Dobrš (also Zo, Mar, Dbrm, IvAl): [...] имѣите солъ въ себѣ и миръ имѣите междѫ собоѫ.

John 7: 7

Cur (fol. 143v, l. 26 – fol. 144, l. 1), Ban: Не можеть мирь ненавыдѣти вась. || <...> ꙗко азь свдѣтельствоуѧ ω немь.[63]

[63] Corrector A has inserted the conjuntion и before ꙗко, has changed свдѣтельствоуѧ to свдѣтельствоуѫ, and has added the missing portion in the top margin. The second half of the insertion (мене же ненавидит, ꙗко дела того лѫкава сѫт) replaces the original version ꙗко дѣла го зла сѧть, which has been crossed out by corrector A.

Dobrš (also Zo, Mar, Ass, Dbrm, IvAl): **Не можеть миръ не видѣти** [*sic*] **вась. мене же не видить**[*sic:* **ненавидитъ**] **ꙗко азъ свѣдѣтелъствоуѫ о немъ.**

John 8: 14–16

Cur (f. 146ᵛ, ll. 14–16), Ban: 14 [...] **свⷣѣтель|ство моѥ истино ѥсть** <...>
16 <...> **ꙗко ѥдынь | нѣсьмь.**

Dobrš (also Zo, Mar, Ass, Dbrm, IvAl, all without **то** in verse 16; see discussion of syntactic idiosyncrasies above): 14 [...] **свѣдѣтелъство мое истинънъ** [*sic*] **есть. ꙗко вѣмъ ѡть кѫдоу прїдохъ. и камо идѫ. вы же не вѣсте ѿ кѫдоу идѫ и камо идѫ.** 15 **вы по плъти сѫдите азь не сѫждѫ никомуже** [*sic*]. 16 **аще ли и сѫждѫ азь то сѫдъ мои истиненъ есть. ꙗко единъ нѣсъмъ.**

John 19: 29

Cur (fol. 169ʳ, ll. 19–20), Ban: [...] **сьсѧдь же стоꙗше пльнь ѡць|та.** <...> **и вь трьсть вьньзьши.**

Dobrš (also Zo, Mar, Ass, Dbrm, IvAl, Kox): [...] **съсѫдъ же стоꙗше плънъ ѡцта: и напльньше гѫбѫ ѡцта: и на тръсть възьньше:**

The following omission is, in addition, shared by the Koxno Gospel:

John 14: 9–10

Cur (fol. 160ʳ, ll. 11–13), Ban, Kox: 9 [...] **и не позна ли мене филипе. вы|дѣвви мѧ выдѣ**<**вь**> **ѡц҃а.** <...> 10 **не вѣроуѥши | ли ꙗко азь вь ѡц҃и и ѡц҃ь вь мнѣ** [...][64]

Dobrš (also Zo, Mar, Ass, Dbrm, IvAl): 9 [...] **не позна ли мене филипе. видѣвыи мѧ видѣ ѡц҃а како ты гл҃ешъ покажи || намь ѡц҃а.** 10 **не вѣроуеши ли. ꙗко азъ въ ѿц҃и и ѡтецъ въ мнѣ.** [...]

That the Curzon Gospel books of Mark, Luke, and John were not copied directly from the Banica Gospel is indicated by numerous omissions of standard text in the Banica version alone. The following are a few examples of such omissions.

[64] The last two letters in **выдѣ**<**вь**> have been erased and replaced by corrector A with a superscript **л** and the word **еⷭ** (**выдѣⷧ еⷭ**). The corrector has also inserted a superscript **н** over **мѧ** (**мⷩѧ**) and a superscript **т** over **ѡц҃ь** (**ѿць**) and has placed a semicolon after **мене**. The missing portion has been added in the right-hand margin, apparently also by corrector A, and appears now as **и како ти | гл҃ши по|жи нⷨ| ѡц҃а** (It appears that the second, third, and fourth lines of this insert, which has been written close to the right-hand edge of the vellum, originally contained one or more additional letters which were subsequently lost when the folios were trimmed during binding and gilding at some time prior to the Museum's acquisition of the manuscript.)

Mark 6: 16–17

Cur (fol. 53ʳ, l. 26 – fol. 53ᵛ, l. 3; also Dobrš, Zo, Mar, Ass, Dbrm, IvAl): 16
слышаѧвь же иродь реⷱ. ѥгоже азь. ‖ оусѣкн<а>хь иѡⷩа сьи ѥсть. тьи вьста ѿ| мрьтвихь. 17 Тьи бо иродь пославь ѧти | иѡⷩа.[65]

Ban: 16 слышав же ироⷣ реⷱ. ѥгоже | азь оусѣкнѫхь иѡана тьи ѥсть. <...>
17 Тьи бо ироⷣ | пославь ѫть иѡана.

Mark 12: 20–1

Cur (fol. 66ʳ, l. 24 – fol. 66ᵛ, l. 1; also Dobrš, Zo, Mar, Dbrm, IvAl): 20 вѣ
же .з҃. братеи. и прьвы поѧ|ть женѧ. и ꙋмираѧ не ѡставить сѣмене. | 21 и
.в҃. поѧть ѧ. и ꙋмрѧть[66] и ть и не ѡста‖вить сѣмене. и г҃ такожⷣе.

Ban: 20 вѣ | же .з҃. братиѧ. и прьвы поѫть женѫ. и оу|мираѫ не остави сѣмене. 21 <...> и трети тако|жⷣе.

Luke 8: 35

Cur (fol. 94ʳ, ll. 6–8; also Dobrš, Zo, Mar, Ass, Dbrm, IvAl, Plov): изыдошѧ вы|дѣти бывшаго. и придошѧ кь іⷭви. и ѡбрѣтошѧ сѣдѧща чл҃вка.

Ban: и изыдошѫ видѣти быв’шаго. <...> и обрѣтошѫ | сѣдѧща чл҃вка.

Luke 8: 45

Cur (fol. 94ᵛ, ll. 9–11; also Dobrš (оугнѣтаѥть Ø), Zo, Mar, Ass, Dbrm, IvAl, Plov): [...] реⷱ петрь и|же сь нимь бѣхѧ. наставниче народь оу|тѣшнѣѥть тѧ. и гнететь.

Ban: [...]реⷱ петрь и иже бѣхѫ сь ним’. | <...> нароⷣ оутѣшнѣѥть тѧ и гнететь.

John 1: 22–3

Cur (fol. 131ʳ, ll. 22–5, also Dobrš, Zo, Ass, Dbrm, IvAl; folio missing from Mar): 22 рекошѧ же ѥмоу кто ѥси ты. да | ѿвѣть дами пославши[67] ни. что
гл҃ѥ|ши ѡ тебѣ самомь. 23 реⷱ же азь глаⷭ вь|пиѧщаго вь поустини.

[65] There is an illegible erased letter, mostly likely а, under the jus in what now appears as оусѣкнѫхь. The jus, written by corrector B, appears to be ѫ, which this corrector generally uses where ѫ would be expected in canonical Old Church Slavonic. As it lacks the top horizontal stroke that is characteristic of corrector B's ѫ it may be interpreted alternatively as ѫ although no other examples of ѫ appear in corrector B's hand. The initial letter с in слышаѧвь has been retraced later in red ink. The first half of verse 17 has been erased and recopied, apparently by the primary original scribe.

[66] Corrected to ꙋмреть by corrector B.

[67] Corrector A also has had a hand in this passage, adding a cursive supercript м to пославши (пославшиⷨ), inserting the word ѥⷭ at the end of the sentence, and changing ѧ to ѫ (рекошѫ, вь|пиѫщаго).

Ban: 22 ѹекошѫ же ѥмꙋ кто є|си ты. да ѿвѣть дамы пославшимь ныи <...> |
23 Рє^{ч} же азь гла^{с} вьпиѫщаго вь поустыни.

John 15: 12–13

Cur (fol. 161^{v}, l. 25 – fol 162^{r}, l. 2; also Dobrš, Zo, Mar, Ass, Dbrm, IvAl,
Kox): 12 Се же ѥ|сть заповѣдь моѧ. да любыте дроу||гь дроуга. ꙗко и^{же}
азь вьзлюбихь ви. 13 Бо|льшѧ се [*sic*] любве. никтоже не имать. [...] |[68]

Ban: 12 Се же ѥсть заповѣдь моꙗ. да | любите дроугь дроуга. <...>
большѫѫ сеѫ любьве никтоже не имать. [...]

Conversely, similar omissions of text from the Curzon Gospel manuscript indicate that it was not the protograph for the Banica Gospel. The homoeoteleuton in the first example below also occurs in the Dobrejšo Gospel:

Mark 8: 22

Cur (fol. 57^{v}, ll. 23–4), Dobrš (приде): И приве|<де> [*sic*][69] витьсаидѧ. <...>
и млѣхѧ и да коснеть.

Ban (also Zo, Mar, Dbrm, IvAl): И приide їсь в|ь вит'саидѫ. и приведошѫ
кь немꙋ | слѣпаго. и млѣхѫ и да и коснеть.

Luke 8: 2

Cur (fol. 92^{r}, ll. 18–20): 2 и жени ѥтери иже вѣхѧ исцѣлени ѿ рань | и
недѧгь. и дхь зьль. и болѣзны. <...> 3 из неѧже седьмь вѣсь изыде.

Ban (also Zo, Mar, Dbrm IvAl; folio missing from Dobrš): 2 и жены ѥтеры
ѫже вѣхѫ исцѣле|ны. ѿ недѫгь и рань. и дхь зьль и болѣзни. | мариа
нарицаѥмаꙗ магдалини. 3 из не|ѫже седьмь вѣсь изыде.

The defective passage cited below from the Curzon Gospel is otherwise consistent with the Zo, Mar, IvAl tetraevangelion version, while the Banica Gospel, which shares the omission, and the Dobromir Gospel both follow the lectionary tradition by inserting the phrase имѣѫи оуши слы|шати да слышить that appears earlier in Luke 8:8. Both the Banica Gospel and the Codex Marianus, however, omit the expected phrase се глѧ възглаcи:

[68] The ѧ in моѧ has been erased and altered to а (моа), apparently by corrector A, who has added a superscript ѫ to Бо|льшѧ (Бо|льш^{ѫ}ѧ) and an apostrophe to любве (люб'ве).

[69] A superscript де has been added in red ink to the line-end fragment приве, apparently by corrector B, and the е has been corrected in red ink to ь forming при^{де}вь; in connection with this, the original де that begins the following line has been erased, resulting in при^{де}вь| витьсаидѧ.

Luke 8: 15 (folio missing from Dobrš)

Cur (fol. 93ʳ, ll. 3–5): [...] **иже добромь ср^д^цемь.** <...> **слышаѧжще | слово дрьжѧть. и плодь творѧть** [*sic*] **вь трьпѣ|ни.** <...> {<u>ко^ц^</u> <u>не^д^</u> [...]}

Ban [...] **и|же добромь ср^д^цемь.** <...> **слышѫще слово дрьжѫть. | и пло^д^ творѧть вь трьпѣни.** <...> **имѣѫи оуши слы|шати да слышить.** {**ко^ц^. не^д^** [...]}

Ass, Dbrm, Plov: [...] **іже добромъ | срдцмъ и благо|мъ. слъишѧще | слово дръжѧт. | и плодъ творѧтъ | въ тръпѣніи. | Ѥі гл҃ѧ възгла|сі. Имѣѭи. оуши | слъышати да | слъышітъ .·.**

Mar (omitted last phrase **се гл҃ѧ възгласи** later added in margin), Zo, IvAl: [...] **іже добромь | сръдьцемъ и благомь. слъі|шавъше слово дръжѧтъ. і пло|дъ творѧтъ въ тръпѣнии.** <...> **.·.**

John 9:22

Cur (fol. 149ᵛ, ll. 17–20): **сего ради рекоста | родителѣ нго зане боꙗста сѧ юдеѧ. |** <...> **да аще кто исповѣсть** <**іс^с^ь**>[70] **х^с^а. да бѧде|ть ѿлѧчень ѿ сьборища.**

Cf. Ban (also Dobrš, Zo, Mar, Ass, Dbrm, IvAl, all without **сь**): **сего ради родителѣ нго рекоста. | зане боꙗста сѧ июдеи. юже бо сѧ бѣхѫ свѣ|щали сь** [*sic*] **июдеи. да аще кто исповѣсть х^с^а. | да бѫдеть ѿлѫчень ѿ сьборища.**

4

In contrast to the shared versions of Mark, Luke, and John (which correspond fairly closely to the Dobrejšo Gospel), the Curzon and Banica versions of Matthew differ from each other quite noticeably. Since, as suggested by Conev, the Banica version of Matthew does not derive from the protograph for the Dobrejšo Gospel,[71] it can be assumed that the Banica version was taken from a replacement source that did not originally accompany the other three books. On the other hand, while the Curzon version of Matthew contains a number of peculiarities which make it difficult to determine its textological affiliation, it does appear to have more than one protograph. The second half of the Curzon version of Matthew, beginning around Chapter 16, is closer to the Dobrejšo version than to any of the other versions compared here.

[70] The Curzon Gospel is alone in adding **іс^с^ь**. This word subsequently has been erased, presumably by corrector A, in conjunction with the addition of the omitted text, but it is still legible. The point after **х^с^а** has been changed to a comma by corrector A, who also has changed **ѧ** to **ѫ** (**бѫде|ть, ѿлѫчень**) and has inserted the omitted text into the lower margin (**сьвещаш^е^ бо иѹдеи ꙗко**).

[71] Conev, 'Knižovni starini' (n. 5), 25. However, a shared source is noted only for Mark and Luke.

In addition, it is somewhat more consistent lexically than the Banica version of Matthew with the Curzon and Banica Mark, Luke, and John. From about Chapter 25 to the end of Matthew, both the Curzon and Dobrejšo Gospels share a number of lexical and textual variants with the Plovdiv Gospel and, to a lesser extent, the Ostromir Gospel (abbreviated as Ostr).[72] Where the Curzon Gospel diverges from the Dobrejšo Gospel in this portion, it is the Curzon version, rather than the Dobrejšo version, that tends to coincide with the Plovdiv Gospel. These facts suggest both multiple protographs for the Curzon version of Matthew and some degree of lectionary influence for at least this part of the text. In contrast, the first portion of Matthew in the Curzon Gospel, up to about Chapter 16, differs from both the Banica Gospel and the Dobrejšo Gospel; here its textual divergences from the Dobrejšo version occasionally coincide with the Tsar Ivan Alexander Gospel (see, for example, Matt. 14: 36 below).

Table 3, which has been compiled on the basis of Horálek's list,[73] offers a few examples of lexical items, all from the second half of Matthew, that are common to both the Curzon and Dobrejšo Gospels and do not have a parallel in the Banica version. These items include several variants that are shared by the Ostromir and Plovdiv lectionaries.

Table 3

водѫ: Matt. 24: 39 (also Zo, Mar; Ban, Ass, Ostr, IvAl, Kox, Plov **потопь**).

жизнь: Matt. 18: 9 (Ban, Zo, Mar, IvAl **жїво^{т}**).

заколена: Matt. 22: 4 (Dobrš **заклана**; Ban **исколени**, also Zo, Mar, Ass, Ostr, IvAl, Kox **исколена**, Plov **исклахь**).

знаменавше: Matt. 27: 66 (also Zo, Mar, Kox, Plov; Ban, Ass, Ostr, IvAl **запечѣтлѣвше**).

земни: Matt. 17: 25 (also Ass, Ostr, Plov; Ban, Zo **зем'сти**; Mar, IvAl, Kox **земьсции**).

ини: Matt. 26: 67 (Ban, Zo, Mar, Ass, Ostr, IvAl, Kox, Plov **ѡви**).

кь дынѣ: Matt. 26: 18 (also Ass; Ban, Zo, Mar, Plov **кь ѥтероу**, IvAl **къ ѡнсици**).

[72] Citations here are from N. N. Rozov *et al.* (eds.), *Ostromirovo evangelie: 1056–1057 goda* (L.–M., 1988). Reference is not made to the Dobromir Gospel in this section, as its text of Matthew has been lost (with the exception of the nine folios mentioned in n. 31 above).

[73] Horálek, *Evangeliáře* (n. 37), 80–100.

напитѣхомь: Matt. 25: 37 (Dobrš **питахомь**; also Ostr, Kox, Plov; Ban **натрѹдихомь**[*sic*], Zo, Mar, Ass **натроухомъ**, IvAl **накръмихωмъ**).

невръгше: Matt. 22: 5 (also Ostr, and Plov **невръгошѧ**; Ban, IvAl **не ражьдьше**; Zo, Mar, Ass, Kox **не рождъше**).

свѣть сьтворишѧ: Matt. 26: 4 (also Zo, Mar; Ban, Ass, IvAl, Kox **свѣщашѫ**; Ostr **съвѣщашѧ сѧ**; phrase omitted from Plov).

трищи: Matt. 26: 34 (Ban, Zo, Mar, Ass, IvAl, Ostr, Kox, Plov **три краты**).

оучителиѥ, оучитель: Matt. 23: 7, 8 (also Ass, Kox; Ban, Zo, Mar, Ostr, IvAl, Plov **рав'ви, рав'ви**).

хоулы: Matt. 15: 19 (Ban, Zo, Mar, IvAl **власвимиѧ**).

That the protograph for the Banica Gospel's version of Matthew differs from the protograph for its version of Mark, Luke, and John, as well as from all portions of Matthew in the Curzon Gospel, is suggested by the Banica version's use of **съньмище** and **сънъмъ** (also Zo, Mar, Ass, Ostr, IvAl, Kox, Plov) instead of expected **съборище** and **съборъ**, the forms that appear in the Curzon and Dobrejšo versions of Matthew, and in the Banica and Curzon Gospel versions of Mark, Luke and John (Matthew 9: 35 (folio missing from Dobrš), 10: 17, 12: 9, 13: 54, 23: 6, 23: 34, 26: 59). The Curzon Gospel shares with the Dobrejšo Gospel the preposition **на** rather than expected **въ**, with **сьборище/сборище** in Matt. 10: 17 and 23: 6 (the latter in the hand of the secondary original scribe). Significant too is the parallel sandwiching of the variants **пропѧтиѥ** and **пропеньше** in Matt. 27: 31, 35 between two instances of **распнѧть** in Matt. 27: 26 and 27: 38:

	Matt. 27: 26	27: 31	27: 35	27: 38
Cur, Dobrš	**распнѧть**	**пропѧтиѥ**	**пропеньше**	**распнѧть**
Ban	**пропнѫть**	**распѧтиѥ**	**пропнѫшѫ**	**пропѧщѫ** [*sic*]
Mar	**пропънѫтъ**	**пропѧтие**	**пропьньше**	**пропѧшѧ**
Zo	**распьнѫтъ**	**распѧтие**	**пропьнъше**	**распѧшѧ**
Ass, Ostr, IvAl, Kox, Plov:	**распьнѫтъ**	**распьѧтіе**	**распеньше**	**распьѧсѧ/распѧшѧ**

As in Luke and John, so in Matthew the Curzon Gospel shares with the Dobrejšo Gospel the variant **коурѧ**, while the Banica Gospel has **пѧтель**. Worth noting too is the fact that in Matthew it is the Koxno Gospel that uses **алекторь**, not the Curzon Gospel (unfortunately, none of the relevant passages outside Matthew appears in the Koxno Gospel).

Cur, Dobrš	Ban	IvAl	Plov	Kox	Zo	Mar	Ass, Ostr
Matt. 26: 34							
коурѧ	пѧтель	пѧт<е?>лъ[74]	пѧтель	пѧтель	коуръ	кокотъ	коуръ
Matt. 26: 74							
коурѧ	пѧтель	пѧтелъ	пѧтель	алекторь	коуръ	кокотъ	коуръ
Matt. 26: 74							
коурѧ	пѧтель	пѧтелъ	пѧтель	алекторь	коуръ	кокотъ	коуръ

The following are examples of textual parallels between the second portion of the Curzon Gospel's version of Matthew and the same part of the text in the Dobrejšo Gospel. The distribution of the oppositions книгъчиѧ / книжьници and ни [...] оставлꙗѥте / възбранꙗѥте in Matt. 23: 14 is characteristic of the general distribution of textual variants among the four tetraevangelia compared here:

Cur, Dobrš: книжници

IvAl: книжници

Ban: книгочиѫ

Zo, Mar: кънигъчиѧ (Mar къникь|чиѩ)

Cur, Dobrš: и хотѧщи|мь внити. вьзьбранѣѥте

IvAl: ни вьхо|дѧщихъ ѡставлѣете

Ban: и вьходѧщиⷯ не ѡставите внити

Zo, Mar: ни въхо|дѧщихъ оставѣете вънити

Matt. 16: 22

Cur (fol. 19r, ll. 20–1), Dobrš: Петрь же начѧть прѣрицати | ѥмоу
Ban, Zo, Mar, IvAl: И поѥмь петра и начѧть прѣрѣкати ѥмȣ

The second of the two omissions shown below (from the last part of Matthew) is shared by the Plovdiv Gospel:

Matt. 25: 35–6

Cur (fol. 36v, ll. 8, 10), Dobrš (also without сѧ): 35 вьзальках҄ь бо <...> и дасте ми ꙗсти. [...] 36 <...> болѣⷯ и посѣтисте мѧ.

[74] This word now appears as пѧтьлъ. The ь seems to be a correction by a later hand of an illegible erased letter, most likely е. The ъ is a correction from ь, apparently by the original scribe. The right margin contains an erasure, of which the visible portion, in a different later hand, appears to be а<--->ⷮорь, with either two or three illegible letters (possibly алекⷮорь).

Plov: 35 **вьзьал'кахь** [*sic*] **во | сѧ. <не?> дасте ми ꙗсти** [...] 36 <...> **воленъ вѣхь и <не> посѣтисте мѧ.**
Ban, Zo, Mar, Ostr, Ass, IvAl, Kox: 35 **вьзал'ках во сѧ и дасте ми ꙗ|сти.** [...] 36 **нагь и ѡдѣ|ꙗсте мѧ. волѣхь и посѣтисте мѧ.**

Table 4 (again based primarily on Horálek's list)[75] offers a few examples of lexical variants from the Curzon Gospel's version of Matthew that are not shared by either the Banica or the Dobrejšo Gospels. The lexical divergences are distributed over both halves of the text:

Table 4

вьзмѧтоше: Matt. 14: 26 (Ban, Dobrš, Zo, Ostr, IvAl, Kox, Plov **смѫтѫшⷭѫ**; Mar, Ass **съмѧшѧ сѧ**).

десите: Matt. 22: 9 (Ban, Dobrš, Zo, Ass, Ostr, IvAl, Kox, Plov **ѡбрѧщете**).

заблѧжⷣьшаго: Matt. 18: 11 (also Kox, Plov; Ban, Dobrš, Zo, Mar, Ass, Ostr, IvAl **погывшаго**).

кѧпини: Matt. 7: 16 (Ban **триволѣ**, Ass **тривола**; Zo, Mar, Ostr, IvAl **рѣпьѣ**; Kox **тривонь**; folio missing from Dobrš; τρίβολος).

льна: Matt. 12: 20 (Ban **плета**; Dobrš, Ass, IvAl **плата**: Zo, Mar **пръта**; Ostr **пърта**; Kox **прьⷭта** [*sic*]).

лѧкавы: Matt. 25: 26 (also Kox; Ban, Dobrš, Zo, Ass, IvAl, Ostr **лѣниве**; Mar **лѣнъı**; Plov **невѣрны**.

масла: Matt. 25: 3, 4 (also IvAl; Ban, Dobrš, Zo, Mar, Ass, Kox **ѡлѣꙗ**; Ostr **елѣа**; Plov **ѥлеꙗ, ѡлѣи**); cf. Matt 25: 8 **ѿ ѡлѣꙗ** (IvAl **ѿ масла**).

ѿлѧчѣѥть сѧ: Matt. 15: 8 (Ban, Dobrš, Zo, Mar **ѿстоить**).

силенъ: Matt. 14: 30 (also IvAl; Ban, Dobrš, Zo, Mar, Ass, Ostr, Dbrm, Kox, Plov **крѣпькь**).

стьльзь: Matt. 22: 19 (Ban **сьнѫзы** [*sic*], folio missing from Dobrš; Zo, Mar **скълѧзъ**; Plov **скилези**; Ass, IvAl, Kox **образь**; Ostr **цѧтѫ**).

тмѧ кромѧшнѧѫ: Matt. 25: 46 (also Plov; cf. Ban, Dobrš, Zo, Mar, Ass, Ostr, Kox **мѫкѫ вѣчнѫѫ**; this portion of the text is missing from IvAl).

храмь бж҃и: Matt. 12: 4 (also Zo, Mar, IvAl; cf. Ban, Dobrš **домь б҃и**).

чѣⷭ: Matt 14: 25 (Ban, Dobrš, Zo, Mar, Ass, Ostr, IvAl, Kox, Plov **стражѫ**).

While the lexical divergences from the other manuscripts are distributed over the whole of Matthew, textual anomalies are confined mainly to the portion preceding chapter 16. At least some idiosyncrasies may be the product of the scribe's attempt to deal with an illegible protograph, but a comprehensive

[75] Horálek, *Evangeliáře* (n. 37), 80–100.

investigation may yield another explanation. One example of a textual anomaly distinguishing the Curzon Gospel from the rest of the manuscript versions examined is the choice of the verb in the phrase прѣити на ѡнь поль in Matt. 14: 22 (fol. 15^{v}, l. 24) for expected варити (Ban, Dobrš, Zo, Mar, Ass, IvAl, Plov, Kox; ἐμβῆναι εἰς τὸ πλοῖον). Another anomaly is вєⷱроу жє бывшоу in Matt. 14: 15 on the same page (fol. 15^{v}, l. 8) for expected поздѣ жє бывшоу (Ban, Dobrš, Zo, Mar, Ass, Ostr, IvAl, Kox, Plov). A number of idiosyncrasies occur in Matt. 14: 26–7, including the imperative плаваитє for expected дрьзаитє:

Cur (fol. 16^{r}, ll. 6–9): 26 [...] и | вьзмѧтошє сѧ гл̂ѧщє. что сєи ѥⷭ. ѿ | страхѧ вьзьпишѧ. 27 авиѥ іcⷭь рєⷱ имь пла|ваитє аз ѥсьмь. нє воитє сѧ.

Ban (also Dobrš, Zo, Mar, Ass, Ostr, IvAl, Kox, Plov (зракь), all with азъ єсьмь. нє воитє сѧ): 26 [...] и смѫтишⷭѫ гл̂ѧщє, | ꙗко призраⷦ ѥⷭ. и ѿ страха вьзьпишѫ | гл̂ѫщє. 27 и авиѥ жє рєⷱ имь і͠сь. дрьза|итє нє воитє сѧ азь ѥсьмь.

In the following excerpt, the Curzon Gospel version even goes so far as to paraphrase the standard Greek text (καὶ παρεκάλουν αὐτὸν ἵνα μόνον ἅψωνται τοῦ κρασπέδου τοῦ ἱματίου αὐτοῦ). Here the Curzon and the Tsar Ivan Alexander Gospels share the variant исцѣлѣшѧ for спасєни бъшѧ:

Matt. 14: 36

Cur (fol. 16^{r}, l. 26 – fol. 16^{v}, l. 2): и мл̂ѣхѧ идѣтє кь || нємоу вьзложить рѧкѧ на нь. ѥлико сѧ | прикоснашѧ кь нємоу исцѣлѣшѧ.

Ban (also Dobrš, Zo, Mar): и мл̂ишѫ и да тькмо прі|коснѫт сѧ вьскрилиє ризь ѥго. ѥ|лико сѧ прикоснѫшѫ. спⷭєні бышѫ:

IvAl (fol. 45^{v}, l. 21 – fol. 46^{r}, l. 1): и молѣахѫ ѥго. | да тъчиѫ прикоснѫт сѧ вьскри|лию ризѣ ѥго. ѥлико жє ихъ при||коснѫ сѧ исцѣлѣшѫ.

The Curzon scribe also appears to have skipped an entire folio from the protograph in copying: fol. 4^{r} ends at Matt. 8: 21 (l. 26: г͠и повєли ми пръжⷣє ити. и погрєсти ||), but the text continues on fol. 4^{v} at approximately Matt. 9: 1 (the first four and a half lines are now missing), the first legible line being at Matt. 9: 2 (l. 5: И сє принєсѧ к нємоу ѡсла|вєнь жилами. на ѡдрѣ лєжѧщь).

* * *

This preliminary report has sought to demonstrate that the Curzon Gospel warrants attention, both in its own right, for its unusual orthographic features and the textual idiosyncrasies of its version of Matthew, and also for its unusually close relationship to the

Banica Gospel, which is indicated by striking coincidences in lexicon, syntax, and general textology between the two manuscripts in Mark, Luke, and John. The Curzon Gospel is thus a potential source of circumstantial evidence on the language and textology of the Banica books of Mark, Luke, and John, and since it can reasonably be dated to the mid-fourteenth century, it can serve as a chronological reference-point for the Banica Gospel, whose dating up to now has been speculative. Moreover, since its books of Mark, Luke, and John are intact, the Curzon Gospel provides a reasonably close version of those folia that are now missing from the Banica Gospel. Palaeographic comparison with a wide variety of other Bulgarian Church Slavonic manuscripts should provide the most reliable basis for determining the precise date and geographic origin of both the Curzon Gospel and the Banica Gospel, and for establishing the place of these two gospels, and of their orthographic systems, within the Middle Bulgarian manuscript tradition.

Cyrillic Printing in Trnava, *c*.1680–1727

By RALPH CLEMINSON

AMONG the less well-known centres of Cyrillic book production in the early modern period the university press at Trnava occupies a special position. Its central geographical situation, even though it is outside the homelands of Cyrillic writing, caused it to become involved with three strands of the Cyrillic printing tradition, the East Slavonic (to which it contributed the first books intended for Subcarpathian Ruthenia), the South Slavonic (specifically that derived from *bosančica*), and the Rumanian. All the books concerned are now very rare. Some of them have been described in detail, but by and large as items on the periphery of the various bibliographical spheres to which they belong. The present study, by contrast, aims to deal with the Cyrillic output of the Trnava press as a whole.

1

The town of Trnava (in Hungarian Nagyszombat) was one of the most important in the Kingdom of Hungary in medieval and early modern times. A royal free town since 1239, it enjoyed considerable economic importance until the eighteenth century. It was also prominent in the ecclesiastical and, consequently, the intellectual life of the country. It was, moreover, one of the few towns in Hungary not to be completely won over by the Reformation.[1] This was one reason why it became an important centre of the Hungarian Counter-Reformation. Another was the fact that in 1543 the dangers resulting from the Turkish invasion had induced the Primate of Hungary, the Archbishop of Esztergom, to remove his residence to Trnava, which remained the archiepiscopal seat until 1820. A third factor was the influence of the Jesuits, who had been active in Trnava since 1561 and, as usual, were much involved in educational activities. Thus it was that in 1635, when Cardinal Péter Pázmány founded a university at Trnava (at this time and for long afterwards the only one in the Kingdom),[2] he placed it

[1] *Dejiny Trnavy*, ed. J. Šimončič and J. Watzka (Bratislava, 1988), 7.

[2] The late fourteenth-century foundations at Pécs and Óbuda had proved short-lived, and the Academia Istropolitana, founded at Pozsony (Bratislava) in the reign of Matthias Corvinus, had fared no better.

under the control of the local Jesuit congregation. The university continued to be run by the Jesuits until the order was suppressed in 1773. In 1777 it was transferred to Buda, and shortly afterwards to Pest, where it survives to this day as the University of Budapest (Eötvös Loránd Tudományegyetem).

The history of printing at Trnava is connected with both the Jesuit order and the University. The first press was established in 1577 by Miklós Telegdy (1535–86), who bought the old Jesuit press at Vienna and transferred it to Trnava. After Telegdy's death in 1586 the press went through various vicissitudes: its ownership was disputed and its equipment was transferred (at least in part) to Pozsony (Preßburg; Bratislava). It was the foundation of the university that restored its fortunes and, although full restitution of its equipment was apparently not achieved until 1648, it began to function as the university press in 1640, and continued to operate in Trnava as long as the university remained there. It was removed to Buda along with the university in 1777.[3]

The period in which the university press operated was more significant than any other in the history of printing in Trnava, and the press's activity was from the first—as might be expected of a Jesuit institution—intimately connected with the Counter-Reformation. The latter made great progress in Hungary in the course of the seventeenth century,[4] and marched hand in hand with the re-establishment of Habsburg power over the country. The Hungarian Counter-Reformation, although largely concerned, as elsewhere, with winning back to Roman Catholicism those areas which had been converted to Protestantism, also affected those subjects of the Hungarian Crown who professed Orthodoxy. These were chiefly the Slavonic population of Subcarpathian Ruthenia, the Rumanians of Transylvania, and the Serbs in the south of the kingdom, all peoples who traditionally used the Cyrillic alphabet for writing. It was for their benefit that a number of books were printed in Cyrillic script at Trnava in the late seventeenth and early eighteenth centuries.

These books are particularly associated with the activity of Cardinal Leopold Kollonich (1631–1707), a statesman and prelate very zealous for the re-Catholicization of Hungary, and equally devoted to the Habsburg cause. It was he who originally provided the Cyrillic type for the Trnava press, and he evidently took a particular interest in the Orthodox minorities, exerting himself particularly to provide an effective Catholic administration for Subcarpathian Ruthenia. Although this region had officially been brought into communion with

[3] *Dejiny Trnavy* (n. 1), 111–12.

[4] *A History of Hungary*, ed. P. F. Sugar, P. Hanák, and T. Frank (London–New York, 1990), 109–10.

Rome in 1646 by the Union of Užhorod (Ungvár), many parishes still remained loyal to Orthodoxy, and the jurisdiction of the Catholic bishop was not very effectively exercised. The Hungarian hierarchy seems to have paid little attention to the region until the late 1680s, when Cardinal Kollonich succeeded in placing the capable John Joseph De Camillis (1641–1706) in charge of it. Born of Greek parents in Chios, then under Genoese rule, De Camillis had studied at the Greek College in Rome, and after working in Albania, and then at Rome as procurator general of the Basilian order, in 1689 he was consecrated Bishop of Sebaste *in partibus* and appointed Vicar Apostolic of Munkács (Mukačeve),[5] where he arrived the following year. Under his administration the Subcarpathian Uniates were finally integrated into the life of the Catholic Church in Hungary, and both their numbers increased and the standard of their ecclesiastical life was considerably raised. These were the conditions in which Cyrillic printed works were provided for the area by the Jesuit typography in Trnava.

It is not now possible to determine the full extent of Cyrillic printing at Trnava. The typography archive accompanied the university to Buda in 1777 and was destroyed there in 1956.[6] The small amount of material among the Acta Jesuitica of the Hungarian National Archive that concerns the Trnava university press[7] contains no information about what it published during the relevant period. Archival and manuscript materials relevant to the history of the university itself[8] are likewise silent on this point. The 1710 sale-catalogue of the press[9] does not even include those Cyrillic books which are known to have been published up to that year. (Presumably they were all sold out by then.) It must be remembered that the press's known Cyrillic output has had a very poor survival rate and that many of its Cyrillic printings were of books (abecedaria, etc.) which by their very nature tend to be ephemeral. There must therefore be a strong possibility that there were printings that have not come down to us.

[5] Munkács did not achieve full diocesan status until 1766. Until then its bishops, though often styling themselves Bishop of Munkács, were in fact consecrated to some see *in partibus infidelium* and subordinated to the Bishop of Eger.

[6] J. M. Kiss, L. Szögi and G. Ujvári, *Az Eötvös Loránd Tudományegyetem Levéltára Repertórium, 1635–1975* (Fejesetek az Eötvös Loránd Tudományegyetem történetéből, x) (Budapest, 1988), 9–10.

[7] Budapest, Magyar Országos Levéltár, E152, 237.d. 12. t.

[8] Comprehensively surveyed in László Szögi, *Egyetemünk történetének levéltári és kézirattári forrásai: tematikus repertórium, 1635–1970* (Fejesetek az Eötvös Loránd Tudományegyetem történetéből, viii) (Budapest, 1982).

[9] *Catalogus librorum qui in Academica Societatis Jesu Typographia venales habentur* (Tyrnaviae, 1710), reproduced in H. Radváni, *Knižné katalógy Univerzitnej kníhtlačiarne v Trnave, I: katalóg z roku 1710* (Trnava, 1974).

The printing-house acquired Cyrillic type not later than 1681[10] through the munificence of Cardinal Kollonich. This is demonstrated by the epistle dedicatory addressed by the 'Typographia Tyrnaviensis, Soc. Jesu' to the Cardinal at the beginning of a collection of sermons by György Káldi (1573–1634) which Kollonich caused to be published at Trnava in 1681.[11] Although well known,[12] the relevant passage is worth quoting again at length to examine its implications more closely:

Sed ne simus multùm peregrinum hâc vice; brevitatis causâ commemoremus nostra propria, quæ *Illustrissima Dominatio Vestra* nobis contulit, & per nos, inopiâ librorum laborantibus Parochis; quibus ut esca suppetat, Rationalibus oviculis exibenda, voluit *Illustrissima Dominatio Vestra* libros gratis suppeditari; dato nobis in hunc finem memorabili subsidio. Prospectum insuper voluit *Illustrissima Dominatio Vestra* desertissimis Ruthenorum, ac Rascianorum Animabus, quas ruditate obscurissimas illustrare satagit, procuratis in Ruthenicum Typum magna liberalitate calculis, numquam hic anteà visis. Hos verò in *Illustrissima Dominatione Vestra* abs[que] dubio à Linguarum Donatore Spiritu Sancto profisci conatûs; en manifestum indicium: nam non Latinos tantùm, sed & Germanicos, & Ruthenicos, jamq[ue] etiam Vngaricos pro Dei Gloria resonare per Orbem characteres jussit *Illustrissima Dominatio Vestra*.

[But lest we be too prolix on this occasion, let us for the sake of brevity call to mind our own benefits, which Your Eminence has bestowed upon us, and through us upon parishes suffering from lack of books, which Your Emininence desired to be furnished with books free of charge in order that there should be nourishment to offer to the rational [i.e. human] flock, to which end you gave us memorable assistance. Moreover Your Eminence desired to make provision for the utterly forsaken souls of the Ruthenians and Serbs, which, sunk as they are in the darkness of ignorance, you are at great pains to enlighten, by procuring, with great generosity, type for Ruthenian printing, which has never been seen in these parts before. Your Eminence was without doubt moved to these efforts by the Giver of Tongues, the Holy Ghost. Behold clear evidence of it: for Your Eminence has commanded not only Latin, but German, and Ruthenian, and now also Hungarian letters to resound throughout the world to the glory of God.]

The point of the last sentence is that the Káldi volume was the first Hungarian book sponsored by Kollonich; its importance here, however, depends on whether it can be taken to imply that the Cyrillic

[10] Not 1696 as H. Radváni, *Chorvatské, rumunské, srbské a ukrajinské knihy vytačené v Trnave do konca 18. storočia* (Trnava, 1972), 1, and J. Valach, *Staré tlačiarne a tlačiari na Slovensku* (Martin, 1987), 75, would have it.

[11] György Káldi, *Istennek szent akarattya* [...] Kollonicz Leopold [...] ki-adatta [...] (Nagyszombatba, 1681). For a description, see K. Szabó, *Régi Magyar Könyvtár*, 3 vols. (Budapest, 1879–98), i. no. 1268.

[12] It was quoted in J. Németh, *Memoria typographiarum inclyti regni Hungariae et magni principatus Transsylvaniae* (Pest, 1818), 155–6, and has been referred to repeatedly since.

type had actually been used at this date. The text is not conclusive, and by its very nature may have a tendency to magnify the Cardinal's accomplishments, but it may be doubted whether Kollonich would have supplied the type without some definite project for its use, and the fifteen-year interval between the acquisition of the type and the first demonstrable Cyrillic printing is certainly suspicious. However, these are no more than matters of probability: there is no actual evidence that there was Cyrillic printing at Trnava in the early 1680s, and the most that can be said is that it would not be surprising if there had been.

A further point which appears from the dedication is that there had been no Cyrillic printing in the region before Kollonich's donation. This would seem to be contradicted by references in the bibliographies to a Rumanian catechism printed at Pozsony in 1636;[13] however, all references to this are derived from an entry in the diary of Dr György Dobronoky (1588–1649), the first rector of the university, which reads: '2. Febr. [1636] ... Accepi e Karan Sebes a nostris patribus catechismum P. Canisii e latino in linguam Valachicam imprimendum Posonii opera p. Jacobi Nemethi.'[14] ['I have received from our fathers in Caransebeş the catechism of P. Canisius (translated) from Latin into Rumanian (and) to be printed at Pozsony through the efforts of Fr. Jakob Némethi.'] If Dobronoky had written 'impressum' rather than 'imprimendum', this would indeed constitute evidence that the book had been printed, but as it is it seems more likely that the intention was never carried out and that Kollonich's Cyrillic type was indeed the first in the area.

Where Kollonich acquired the type is not known. Stryps'kyj's conjecture,[15] repeated as fact by later authors,[16] that it came from Cracow seems completely unfounded, as there does not appear to have been any Cyrillic printing at Cracow since the time of Švajpolt Fiol's press at the end of the fifteenth century. It is probably better to accept the evidence of a letter from Kollonich's secretariat to De Camillis, written probably in 1689, that it was made to order for the Cardinal.[17]

[13] Ján Čaplovič, *Bibliografia tlačí vydaných na Slovensku do roku 1700*, 2 vols. (Martin, 1972–84), no. 309.

[14] J. Müller, 'Materialen zur Kirchengeschichte Siebenbürgens und Ungarns im siebzehnten Jahrhundert', *Archiv des Vereines für siebenbürgische Landeskunde*, NS xix (1884), 629. Jacobus Némethi SJ (1573–1644) was indeed involved with the press at Pozsony intermittently from 1625, but he does not seem to have left any published work. See L. Lukács, *Catalogi personarum et officiorum Provinciae Austriae S.I., II (1601–1640)* (Romae, 1982), 688, and J. Szinnyei, *Magyar írók*, 14 vols. (Budapest, 1891–1914), ix, cols. 949–50.

[15] Beloň Rusínsky [pseudonym of H. Stryps'kyj], 'Trnavská univerzita v službe unionistickej idey', *Pamiatke Trnavskej Univerzity, 1635–1777* (Trnava, 1935), 246.

[16] For example, J. Valach, op. cit. (n. 10), 75.

[17] 'Circa li libri da stamparsi in lingua schiavona e rutena, haverà la stampa in Tirnavia, che sta nell' Ungaria Superiore al suo servito, havendo il Sign. Card. de Kolonitz fatto fare i caratteri.'

The form of the letters, moreover, especially those used in the 1696 Catechism (see below, no. 3), suggests affinities with the southern tradition of printing derived in part from *bosančica* rather than Cracow.

2

Secondary sources refer to twelve Cyrillic printings from Trnava. Six of these are attested by extant copies, while the other six are attended by varying degrees of doubt. All twelve are listed below. Where no extant copy can be located, the title is given in square brackets, and references are given to Čaplovič[18] and to the *Régi Magyar Könyvtár*, volume II[19] (hereafter RMK ii) for those books listed therein.

[1. J. J. De Camillis, Casuistica, 1692.]
The evidence for this book is based on two sources. The first is a passage in the *Obrona věrnomu každomu čelověku* by De Camillis's contemporary Michael Andrella (1637–1710).[20] The passage in question is one of several in this violently polemical work in which passion appears to have got the better of syntax, so the overall sense is not altogether clear, but it does certainly refer to 'поганскую тую римскую, катехесисъ, книжку у Тернаве, ахчв [1692] друкъ'.[21] The second source, written nearly a century later, is the unpublished 'Historia Diocesiana' by Daniel Babila or Babilovič (1730–95), which, according to Duliškovič, refers to a 'Casuistica' published in Trnava in 1692 at the expense of Cardinal Kollonich.[22] Babilovič also appears to be the authority for Lucskay's statement that 'libellus Casus intitulatus, sub Iosepho isto Episcopo typis Tyrnaviensibus anno 1692. editus est.'[23] ['A book entitled *Cases* was published in 1692 by the Trnava printing-house under the same Bishop Joseph.']

It will immediately be noticed that Andrella refers to a *Catechesis* rather than a *Casuistica*, whereas Babilovič, judging by Duliškovič's

Quoted in Nicolaus Nilles, *Symbolae ad illustrandum historiae Ecclesiae Orientalis in Terris Coronae S. Stephani* (Oeniponte [Innsbruck], 1855), 857.

[18] Čaplovič, *Bibliografia* (n. 13).

[19] Szabó, *Régi Magyar Könyvtár* (n.11), ii (Budapest, 1885).

[20] Printed in A. Petrov, *Materialy dlja istorii Ugorskoj Rusi, VII: Pamjatniki cerkovno-religioznoj žizni ugrorussov XVI–XVII vv.* (Sbornik Otdelenija russkogo jazyka i slovesnosti, xcvii, no. 2) (Pgr., 1921).

[21] Ibid. 275.

[22] I. Duliškovič, *Istoričeskie čerty ugro-russkich*, iii (Užhorod, 1877), 25–6.

[23] Michael Lutskay, *Historia Carpato-Ruthenorum*, iii (Budae, 1843), 85. This exceedingly rare work, which has now been reprinted in vols. 11, 13, 14, and 16 of the *Naukovyj zbirnyk Muzeju ukraïns'koï kul'tury u Svydnyku*, also includes De Camillis's diary, but this proves to be of no value for determining what he actually published, being exclusively concerned with diocesan administration.

and Lucskay's reports of his history, does not say that it was actually by De Camillis. (Neither, indeed, does Andrella.) Babilovič, a Ruthenian who had studied in Trnava,[24] does at least supply the plausible detail of Kollonich's patronage, but apart from the date there is nothing to show that they are referring to the same book, or that De Camillis had anything to do with it. While it is true that De Camillis was from the beginning of his episcopacy contemplating the publication of Ruthenian books,[25] the intention must not be taken for the deed, and the evidence is far too tenuous to assert that he or anyone else published a *Catechesis* or *Casuistica* or anything else at Trnava in 1692. The fact that such titles were published at Trnava in other years only makes it seem less likely, to the point where the suspicion arises that Andrella was in fact referring to the *Catechesis* of 1698, but mistook the year, while Babilovič, who could have had access to Andrella's manuscript in the Diocesan Archive at Užhorod, compounded the error by turning it into a *Casuistica*. This too is speculation; however, the balance of probability lies with those who regard the 1692 Casuistica as legendary.[26]

[**2.** P. Canisii Catechismus serbice, 1695.]
The only author to mention this book is Šafárik.[27] Although each time he refers to it he cites the same copies (in the collections of A. Dragosavljević in Vukovar and Miklós Jankovich in Pest), on the first occasion he gives the date as **ахчє** (i.e. 1695 correctly printed in Cyrillic numerals), and the on second as **ахѳє** (substituting **ѳ**, which has the numerical value 9, for **ч**, which stands for 90). This inconsistency, typical of a posthumous work (published four years after Šafárik's death in 1861), suggests that the date 1695 is not reliable. The same mistake in the Cyrillic numeral (the substitution of **ѳ** for **ч**) does in fact occur in the 1696 printing of the catechism, which is dated **҂ахѳѕ**. It is not probable that this mistake should be made, and then corrected, in 1695, and then made again in the same book in 1696. Although absolute proof would require positive identification of one of the copies cited by Šafárik,[28] it would seem probable that what Šafárik actually saw was the 1696 Canisius, and that the date 1695 is a mistake.

[24] K. Zsatkovics, 'A magyarországi oroszok történetírása', *Századok*, xxiv (1890), 570; he returned to Munkács in 1758, where he taught in the school, and from 1772 till his death resided at Užhorod.

[25] Cf. the correspondence quoted in Nilles, *Symbolae* (n. 17).

[26] So H. Sztripszky, 'A hazai Rutének legrégibb nyomtatványai', *Magyar könyvszemle*, NS xix (1911), 248, and A. Gyenis, *A nagyszombati egyetem nyomdája és az unió* (Budapest, 1942), 12.

[27] P. J. Šafárik, *Geschichte der südslavischen Literatur* (Prague, 1865), ii. 215 and iii. 295.

[28] The extensive collections of Miklós Jankovich (1772–1846) were acquired by the Széchényi Library in Budapest in 1833, but neither of the two copies of the 1696 Canisius now in the library belonged to Jankovich. The books that he acquired after 1833 were dispersed after his death. See Jenő Berlász, 'Jankovich Miklós könyvtári gyűjteményeinek kialakulása és sorsa', *Az Országos Széchényi Könyvtár Évkönyve 1970–1971* (Budapest, 1973), 109–73.

3. **КРѦТКѦ ѦЗБѸКВИЦѦ,| И КРѦТѦК | КЄРСТЇѦНСКИ́ |** католичански наѹк. | п. ѿ петра канизиа | дрѹштва имена исѹсова. | Сложѐн ѹ Слависки Иезик. | Притискан по милости Припошовано-|га и Привисокога | Гн҃а **КѦРДИНѦЛѦ КОЛОНИЋѦ.** | Острогонског а арцибискѹпа. | ѹ Тернави Тип. академ. Лито Госп. а҃х҃ѳ҃ѕ҃.

RMK ii. 1844. Čaplovič 2343.

This is the first Cyrillic printing from Trnava attested by extant copies, and the earliest demonstrable use of Kollonich's type. It is significant that this occurred in a year when Kollonich donated 1,000 florins to the press,[29] and that his name appears on the title-page; this implies that these Cyrillic imprints were not a commercial proposition, and were produced only when specifically commissioned.

This is a small book of twenty-three leaves, consisting of three gatherings of eight, the eighth leaf of the third gathering being a pastedown. As is usual with Trnava books, the first five rectos of each gathering (except for the very first page of the book) are signed (e.g. B, B2–B5). There is continuous pagination, а҃-м҃в, from the third recto to the last verso. It contains a Croatian translation of the *Catechismus minimus* of St Peter Canisius (1521–97), preceded, as was frequently the case in editions of this work, by the alphabet and syllables, and followed by a selection of hymns. The text of the catechism showed some variation even during the author's lifetime; the present edition follows in arrangement the later (post-1568) editions of the German (as opposed to Latin) version.[30] This catechism was a favourite text of the Jesuits, written by one of the most prominent members of their order, and was printed by them many times, including numerous editions in various languages at Trnava. A Croatian Latin-script version was also printed there in 1696,[31] but it is a separate translation, linguistically quite distinct.

Previous scholars have referred to this book as a Serbian translation of Canisius, presumably because it is printed in Cyrillic type. However, there were a number of Cyrillic books printed for Croats at this period,[32] using a form of type based on western Cyrillic or *bosančica*. Even though this catechism does not employ all the typographical or orthographical conventions of the generality of these printings, the fact

[29] Joseph Maurer, *Cardinal Leopold Graf Kollonitsch, Primas von Ungarn* (Innsbruck, 1887), 353.

[30] *S. Petri Canisii Catechismi Latini et Germanici*, ed. F. Streicher (Romae–Monachii Bavariae, 1933–4), i. 73*. Texts of some of these are printed ibid. ii. 233–90, and display some minor variations. None corresponds exactly to the 1696 Croatian version.

[31] Čaplovič (n. 13), no. 2342.

[32] I. Babac, 'Main Trends in the Croat Language Question', *Aspects of the Slavic Language Question*, ed. R. Picchio and H. Goldblatt, i (New Haven, 1984), 214–15. I am grateful to Dr C. M. MacRobert for drawing my attention to this reference.

that it is translated into a Croatian (Ikavian) dialect justifies us in including it amongst them.

The alphabet which precedes the catechism proper is given once in capitals and once in lower case, in its normal order, and is followed by a short sequence of two-letter syllables consisting of each consonant in turn followed by the vowels а є и о ȣ (i.e. ба, бє, би, etc.). This section contains a number of typographical features which are not found in the other Cyrillic books printed at Trnava. In part these concern the letters specific to (Serbo-) Croatian Cyrillic. As in both handwritten and printed *bosančica* there is a single letter, ꙉ, standing for both ћ and ђ. The postjotated letters љ and њ have the forms ли and ни, while џ is represented by Ꙇ. This last, however, appears to be confined to the alphabet and syllables, and not to be used in the text of the catechism. Likewise z and ѵ are substituted for ѕ and ч in the alphabet and syllables only. (The second of these is also a feature of *bosančica* printing.) The last letter of the alphabet is щ: there are no jers, jat', or prejotated vowels (though ꙗ is sometimes used in the text, e.g. кєрстꙗнин, p. 1; however, [j] is more usually represented by и, e.g. кєрстианскєн, p. 18). The page with the signature A2, containing the alphabet and the beginning of the syllables, is reproduced, somewhat reduced, in István Käfer, *Az Egyetemi Nyomda négyszász éve (1577–1977)* (Budapest, 1977), 49.

[4. Ferenc Szunyogh, Catechismus valachicus, 1696.]
RMK ii.1864. Čaplovič 2368.

No reference to this work has ever cited an actual copy. It is first referred to in print in 1806 by Katona,[33] who gives a brief biography of Szunyogh and says, specifically, 'Edidit Catechismum Valachicum maiorem Romano catholicum, typo Valachico Tirnaviae 1696. 1726. typo Latino Cibinii 1709.' ['He issued a larger Rumanian Roman Catholic Catechism in Cyrillic script at Trnava in 1696 and 1726 and in Latin script at Sibiu in 1709.'] This passage, however, is never referred to by later bibliographers, whose accounts of Szunyogh all appear to be derived from the unpublished 'Bibliotheca Scriptorum Societatis Jesu olim Provinciae Austriae [. . .] ab anno MDLIV ad nostra tempora'[34] by Mihály Antal Paintner (1769–1822). Publication of this work was announced in a flysheet dated 1 June 1802 by the bookseller Michael Sammer of Veszprém[35] and subscriptions solicited, but it did not take place. Paintner's biography of Szunyogh (on p. 443 of his manuscript) was thus written before Katona's was published, but the two are virtually identical: either Katona had had access to Paintner's

[33] Stephanus Katona, *Historia critica regum Hungariae*, 42 vols. (Buda, 1778–1817), xxxviii. 891.

[34] The manuscript is at Pannonhalma, Főapátsági Könyvtár, MS 118.C.35.

[35] A copy of the flysheet is preserved in the Széchényi Library in Budapest under the shelfmark 405.449.

manuscript, or the two were working from a common source. Neither of them indicates his sources. (The 'K' against Szunyogh's name in the index to Paintner's manuscript (p. 346), which turns out to refer to Katona, is a later addition; evidently Paintner has not given up hope of publication and was keeping his manuscript up to date.)

All references to the 1709 and 1726 editions also lead back ultimately to Paintner, and no copy of these has ever been recorded either. It seems highly unlikely that any of them ever existed. It should be noted that both the Trnava editions are alleged to have appeared in years when the press did indeed produce a Cyrillic catechism, and this may be the origin of the references to Szunyogh's supposed work. Admittedly the words 'Valachicus' and 'maior' apply only to the 1726 catechism, but with Cyrillic books the possibilities for confusion are quite considerable, as may be seen from one of the copies of the 1696 Croatian Canisius in the Széchényi Library, which bears an old inscription declaring it to be an 'Alphabetum Valachicum'!

[**5.** P. Canisii Catechismus illyrice, 1697.]
The existence of this book is also very much open to doubt. It is listed by Kukuljević in his *Bibliografija hrvatska* (no. 77), but this is not a reliable source, as he did not describe the majority of his books *de visu* and relied extensively on second-hand information.[36] Zelliger claimed that there was a copy in the General Seminary in Budapest[37] but there is none there now.[38] It is likely that this is a mistake for the Latin-script version of the catechism, which was indeed reprinted at Trnava in 1697 (Čaplovič 2375, RMK ii.1893).

6. **ЍСПОВѢДА́ИІЕ ВѢ́РЫ. | Зь Повеле́нїѧ Пі́ѧша д҃. Па́пы Ры́мскаго.**

Čaplovič 2394a.
This is preserved in a single copy in the library of Matica Slovenská at Martin (shelfmark SD 47502). It is a bifolium, each leaf measuring 183 mm × 151 mm, containing a Ukrainian translation of the *Bulla supra forma juramenti* of Pope Pius IV (also known as the Tridentine Confession). The text, beginning **Ѧ Ї҆мр҃къ, ста́лымъ Оуּмысломъ вѣ́рѹю, й исповѣдѹю**, and ending **ве́длѹгъ си́лъ мо́ихъ старатисѧ бѹдѹ**, occupies the first two and a half pages; the lower half of the third page is

[36] Tomislav Jakić, 'Kukuljević i njegova bibliografija', appendix to Ivan Kukuljević Sakcinski, *Bibliografija Hrvatska* (Ljubljana, n.d. [*c.*1975]; reprint of the Zagreb, 1860 ed.), vi.
[37] Aloysius Zelliger, *Pantheon Tyrnaviense, bibliographicam continens recensionem operum typis Tyrnaviensibus aa. 1578–1930 editorum* (Tyrnaviae, 1931), 37.
[38] So Professor Vilmos Lenhardt, director of the library of the Péter Pázmány Theological Academy, where the Seminary's collections are now housed, kindly informs me.

occupied by a woodcut of three putti entangled in a scroll with the legend AD MAIOREM DEI GLORIAM, and the fourth page is blank. No place or date of publication is given, but the typeface is beyond any doubt the same as that of the other Cyrillic books from Trnava. Čaplovič dates it 'c.1689', but does not give his reasons. It does, however, seem very much the sort of thing that De Camillis would have found useful in his diocese, and probably dates from the time of his episcopate.

7. **КА́ТЕХИ́СИ́СЪ** | Для́ наоуки Оу́гроро́ускимъ людемъ | зложе́нні́й | ѿ превелебнѣ́йш гдна І́ѡ: **І́ОСИФА**: | **ДЕКАМ** і́ли́ хі́о Еппа **СЕБА́С**: моу-|Ка́чов: и́ про́ч: | **НАМѢ́СНИКА АпАСКОГО** На Люми | Восточн: набжен: | въ Кролевствѣ Оу́горскомъ, и́ его̀ Предѣ́лӑ. | **ПРЕСВѢ**: **ЦЕСА**: и́ **КРОЛЕ**: **МАЕ-|СТАТОУ СОВѢ́Т НИКА**. | вТерна́вѣ ти́пом: академ: ѿдь мене ань-|дре́я Гоерманна, Ро́кꙋ бжго, ахѳи.

RMK ii.1933. Čaplovič 2403.

This is a much more substantial work than the previous ones, being intended not for elementary instruction, but for the use of priests and educated laymen. Catechisms of this type were very much part of the Counter-Reformation tradition.[39] This work survives in a number of copies and has been extensively described by Stryps'kyj and by Magocsi and Strumins'kyj.[40] The typesetters' competence in Cyrillic numerals had evidently not improved since 1696, as there are mistakes in both the date (1698, printed **ахѳи** instead of **ахчи**, again substituting the symbol for 9 for the symbol for 90) and the pagination (in which the numbers **рк-рнѳ** are repeated). This last circumstance has misled Stryps'kyj into disputing Szabó's page-count.[41] In fact Szabó is right: the book contains 412 pages (including the blank leaf at the end), being made up of twenty-five gatherings of eight leaves plus one of six.

[**8.** idem, 1699.]

This edition is mentioned only by Radváni,[42] who cites no copies or previous authorities. Perhaps it is an attempt to make sense of the impossible date 1619 in the 1806 Széchényi catalogue,[43] itself presumably the result of reading the date 1698, incorrectly printed as **ахѳи**, as

[39] Cf. J. Szombath, 'Zásluhy trnavskej univerzity o novú katechetiku', *Pamiatke Trnavskej Univerzity* (n. 15) 187–217.

[40] Sztripszky, 'A hazai' (n. 26), 117–23; Paul R. Magocsi and Bohdan Strumins'kyj, 'The First Carpatho-Ruthenian Printed Book', *Harvard Library Bulletin*, xxv (1977), 292–309.

[41] Sztripszky, 'A hazai' (n. 26), 118, and H. Stryps'kyj [H. Sztripszky], 'Z staršoï pys'mennosty Uhors'koï Rusy', *Zapysky Naukovoho tovarystva im. Ševčenka* (1913), 183.

[42] H. Radváni, *Chorvatské, rumunské, srbské a ukrajinské knihy vytlačené v Trnave do konca 18. storočia* (Trnava, 1972), no. 9.

[43] Sztripszky, 'A hazai' (n. 26), 122.

ахѳі, which would be 1619. (The inexperienced reader would be the more likely to make this mistake as и and ı when used as letters both represent the sound [i].)

9. **БꙊКВАРЪ** | Ѩзыка Славе́ньска. | **ПИСАНІЙ ЧТЄНІѨ** | оучи́тисѧ хотѧ́щїй въ по́-|лезное рꙋковоже́нїе. | в' Тирна́вѣ Типо҃ ака́де҃. Ро-|кꙋ ѿ Ржества Хртова, ҂ахчч | ѿ Їѡа́на Андр. Герьма́н.

RMK ii.1966. Čaplovič 2437.

There is a copy of this book in Budapest University Library.[44] The primer consists of twenty leaves, made up of two gatherings of eight and one of four. There is a single pagination running from the second recto to the last verso, г҃–м҃. The date is given as ҂ахчч (instead of ҂ахчѳ), this time substituting the symbol for 90 for that of 9 (the book was published in 1699) and the thirty-ninth page is numbered лт҃ (the 9 now replaced by 300). The book has none of the typographical features deriving from the Bosnian Cyrillic tradition that are found in the 1696 Croatian Canisius (see above, no. 3).

The primer has been variously attributed to De Camillis and to the Galician priest Ivan Kornic'kyj, the translator of De Camillis's catechism into Ukrainian from the original Latin.[45] In fact, however, it is simply a reprint of the primers printed at Lvov in 1671 and 1692.[46] The Trnava primer reproduces the contents of the Lvov primers very closely (except that, being a Roman Catholic edition, it naturally adds the *filioque* to the Creed). Books from Lvov were extensively used in Subcarpathian Ruthenia at this period,[47] so it is not surprising that one of them should be used as the model for the first primer produced specifically for use in the region.

[44] For a facsimile, see Mychajlo Mol'nar, *Slovaky i ukraïnci* (Bratislava, 1965), 119–58. There is also an extensive description in Sztripszky, 'A hazai' (n. 26), 125–31.

[45] Kornic'kyj was evidently quite prominent among the Uniate clergy of the time, as may be concluded from the fact that Andrella goes out of his way to be rude about him on several occasions. However, Andrella's strictures on his 'expulsion of letters' (Petrov, op. cit. (n. 20), 285), cited by Magocsi and Strumins'kyj (op. cit. (n. 40), 301–2 note 18), have nothing to do with the primer or with any other specific book, being concerned rather with the supposed superiority of the Cyrillic over the Latin alphabet.

[46] See Ralph Cleminson, 'East Slavonic Primers to 1700', *Australian Slavonic and East European Studies*, ii (1988), 1–27, nos. 30, 31. It is impossible to say which of the Lvov editions served as the immediate basis for the Trnava reprint, as the two are virtually identical in content; it is moreover not impossible that there were other editions of the primer reprinted at Lvov which are no longer extant.

[47] See Eszter Ojtozi, 'Itogi i zadači issledovanija vostočnoslavjanskix staropečatnyx knig i slavjanskix rukopisej mestnoj redakcii v severovostočnoj časti Vengrii', *Polata k"nigopis'naja*, vi (1982), 30–9.

[**10.** The second Cyrillic edition of Ferenc Szunyogh's Rumanian catechism, 1726.]

The sources and evidence for this book are exactly the same as those for the 1696 edition, discussed as no. 4 above, and the same conclusions as to the likelihood of its existence must be reached as about that edition.

11. **КѦТЕКИСМȢШЬ** | сав | ꙟвъцътȣръ крещинѣскъ. | ꙟ фѡлосȣль, нѣмȣлȣй рȣсескȣ | динь цара оунгȣрѣскъ. | Датъ афаръ | Пинь | ѿсърдиа, ши ѿстенела Мърiи Салѣ. | **ДОМНȢЛȢИ Д: ЇѠѦН ЇѠСИФЬ.** | **ДЕКѦМИЛИ**, | Iпискȣпȣль Севастȣлȣй, ши аль Мȣнка|чȣлȣи: и про. | Чинȣлȣй преѡцескȣ оуни дин лецеа Гречаскъ | Викаришь апостолическȣ ꙟ цара Оунгȣ-|рѣскъ, Сфинтеи ши ꙟнълцатей ꙟпъръцїй | Ръмȣлȣи Сфетникȣ. | Їаръ акȣмь. | ꙟ фѡлосȣл Нѣмȣлȣи Рȣмънескȣ, ꙟ лимба | рȣмънѣскъ ꙟтоарсъ, ши типърита. | Съмбъта маре, ꙟ Типографiа Ѧкадеми|часкъ. Ѧнȣль дела Хс аѱкѕ.

This is a Rumanian translation of De Camillis's catechism. It is described by Veress from a copy, according to him unique, in the possession of Ioan Pap of Ozun;[48] there is (or was) also one in the Astra library at Sibiu.[49] In size and composition it seems to be exactly the same as the Ukrainian version. The publication of this book presumably indicates that the Ukrainian version has been found useful in Subcarpathian Ruthenia, and that a similar success was expected amongst the Uniates of Transylvania. The intermission of twenty-six years (1700–25) during which there is no record of any Cyrillic printing at Trnava is understandable. The uprising led by Ferenc Rákóczi II, which began in 1703, would have interrupted dealings with both Subcarpathian and Transylvanian Uniates for some years. (In particular, it forced De Camillis, who as an appointee of Cardinal Kollonich's can hardly have been regarded with sympathy by Rákóczi, to withdraw to Prešov, where he spent the last two years of his life.) The death of Cardinal Kollonich in 1707 had also deprived the press of a patron who had taken a particular interest in its Cyrillic imprints. The lack of archival records means that we cannot know the precise circumstances in which the Rumanian version of De Camillis's catechism was produced, but its appearance, together with that of the *Casuistica* of the following year, is indicative of the return of more settled times.

[48] Andrei Veress, *Bibliografia Română-ungară* (Bucharest, 1931), no. 321.

[49] Nicolaŭ Toganŭ, *Catalogulŭ Bibliotecei Asociaţiunei transilvane pentru literatura română şi cultura poporului românŭ* (Sibiu, 1895), 3.

12. **КРА́ТКОЕ** | припа́дковъ мора́лныхъ, и҆лѝ Пра́вныхъ | **СОБРА́НІЕ** | Дх҃овнымъ О҆со́бамъ потре́бное. | И҆мȣ́щее в' себѣ̀ Наȣ́кȣ ѡ҆ Сакраме́нтахъ, ѡ҆ десѧти̑ бж҃їихъ прика́занїѧ, ѡ҆ прика-|за́нїѧ цр҃ко́вныѧ, и҆ ѡ҆ наȣ́ци хр҃тїа́нской, | съ Выкла́домъ Сѵ́мвола, и҆лѝ И҆спови-|да́нїѧ Вѣ́ры правосла́вныѧ Каѳоли́че-|скїѧ, съ Выкла́домъ Мл҃твы: О҆́че | на́шъ: и҆ Бц҃е Дв҃о ра́дȣйсѧ. | Та́кожде: и҆ наȣ́кȣ, съ кра́ткымъ, и҆ Припра́|внымъ по́собїемъ: како подобаетъ ю҆́ноша, | и҆ли невинѧ́тков', в' Вѣ́ри Правосла́вной | наставлѧ́ти | **СОДЕРЖА́ЩЕЕ**. | За Блгослове́нїемъ Превеле́бнѣйшаго Гс҃дна | **ГЕѠ́РГІѦ ГЕННА́ДІѦ ВИЗАНТІѦ** | Е҆п҃па севас: мȣка́чов: и҆ про́ч: на лю́ми | Восто́чнаго Наб҃женства, въ кроле́вствѣ ᲂу҆-|горскомъ, и҆ е҆го Предѣ́лахъ, | **НА́МѢСНИКА А҆ПОСТОЛСКОГО**. | Въ Терна́вѣ тѵпо̑ А҆каде̑: по̑зы ра́ди Преве-|ле́бнаго. и҆ все́чнаго клѵ́рȣ Ȣгрорȣ́скаго, и҆зда́|ное е҃ лѣ́та̀ хв҃а ҂аѱкз. Мц҃а ю҆нїѧ днѧ̀ к҃.

George Gennadius Bizánczy was Bishop of Munkács (or strictly of Sebaste) from 1716 to 1733. Although this book is consistently attributed to him, this attribution is not necessarily reliable. The title-page only asserts that the book was issued with his blessing, not that he was its author. In spite of its title, this is (just) the longest Cyrillic book printed at Trnava, with twenty-six complete gatherings of eight leaves and one of 1 + 5. It is described in detail by Stryps'kyj.[50] It is a work in the same spirit and tradition as De Camillis's Catechism, and was evidently issued for the same purpose, namely the edification of the Ruthenian clergy.

3

There is no record of any Cyrillic printing at Trnava after the 1725 *Casuistica* (no. 12 above), and some time later the Cyrillic type was removed from the press, for we find it in use at Kolozsvár in 1746 to print a Latin primer for Ukrainian speakers, *Elementa Puerilis institutionis in lingua Latina* by Bizánczy's successor Manuil Ol'šavs'kyj.[51]

The six books described above represent the sum of what is known about Cyrillic printing at Trnava. It is by no means certain that they were in fact the only Cyrillic books produced there; it is quite possible

[50] Sztripszky, 'A hazai' (n. 26), 245–8.

[51] Idem, 'Z staršoï pys'mennosty' (n. 41) 192–3. The book is described ibid. 184–8, with illustrations showing the typeface, recognizable as that of the Trnava editions. In composition the book evidently owes a considerable amount to the Ukrainian and Belorussian Church Slavonic primer tradition.

that some items have disappeared without trace, just as the undated confession (no. 6 above) had been completely forgotten until the comparatively recent discovery by Čaplovič of the single copy now known. It is possible that other such discoveries will yet be made, but it seems unlikely that any of them will confirm the existence of any of the six unattested printings mentioned in the literature. It is more probable that none of these ever existed.

In spite of its importance as a producer of books in Latin script, the Trnava press stands on the margins of Cyrillic bibliography. For this reason a remarkable amount of legend and inaccuracy has accumulated about its Cyrillic output, and this has been extremely persistent in the literature.[52] It is to be hoped that the ascertainable facts about Cyrillic printing at Trnava assembled here will facilitate a more complete assessment of its importance. This is, after all, not insignificant. Four of the items printed there—the confession (no. 6), the catechism (no. 7), the primer (no. 9), and the *Casuistica* (no. 12)—represent the first four printed works intended specifically for the population of Subcarpathian Ruthenia, and constitute a landmark in the cultural development of that region. The 1696 Canisius is an interesting example of Croatian Cyrillic printing, and represents an isolated example of a book evidently derived from the mainstream of books printed by the Bosnian Franciscans at Venice, but not entirely within that tradition. Finally the Rumanian translation of De Camillis's catechism illustrates very clearly how the cosmopolitan nature of the Trnava community was reflected in its printing activities. Taken together the six books show how a Western press, in this case driven by the impetus of the Counter-Reformation, could produce Cyrillic books for a number of different communities with their own book culture, blending with them its own Jesuit tradition. Here Trnava may take its place alongside other Western centres of Cyrillic printing from Stockholm to Venice, and be seen to have made an individual contribution to the cultural cross-currents between East and West which are found at the centre of European civilization.

[52] There has even been a recent manifestation of the phantom printing house of Körtvélyes (in P. Király, 'Rusinskie izdanija Trnavskoj universitetskoj tipografii', *Russika: sbornik statej, posvjaščënnyj pamjati Èmilja Baleckogo*, ed. M. Péter and B. Tatár (Budapest, 1983), 41) despite its seemingly definitive exorcism by Stryps'kyj (H. Sztripszky, 'Volt-e könyvsajtó a máramorosi Körtvélyesen?', *Hajnal* (Ungvár), ii (1942), 5–34). For the history of this particular mare's nest, see Magocsi and Strumins'kyj, op. cit. (n. 40), 299–300 note 14.

Russian Diplomats on the Future of the European Possessions of the Ottoman Empire: A Document of September/October (Old Style) 1903

By V. V. ZAITSEV

THE extensive domains of the Ottoman Empire situated at the junction of Europe, Asia, and Africa were practically always affected by the movement for national liberation. This circumstance, coupled with the economic and strategic importance of the region, constantly attracted the attention both of the Great Powers and of the independent states of the Balkan peninsula. For the latter the European provinces of the Porte were the target of national propaganda among populations consisting of their own racial and religious kin which they expected to inherit from the legacy of the declining Ottoman Empire, 'the sick man of Europe'. Foreseeing the probability of territorial changes in the Balkan peninsula, the Great Powers wished to reach an understanding on the principles of their Balkan policy. The initiative was taken by those powers that were most deeply interested in the region, namely Russia and Austria-Hungary. This resulted in the bilateral agreement of 1897, supported by the other Great Powers, to uphold the principle of the status quo in the Balkan peninsula. This agreement enabled Russia and Austria-Hungary to gain time for the preparation of a solution of the eastern question in accordance with their interpretation.

The leading Russian diplomats, though convinced of the expediency of the agreement, had varying opinions of its prospects. The greatest optimism was expressed by one of its authors, the Russian ambassador in Vienna, Count Petr Aleksandrovich Kapnist. He considered that it would be a long time before the internal problems of Austria-Hungary allowed her to pursue an active foreign policy. He suggested that use be made of this factor, in conjunction with the bilateral agreement, to change the orientation of Vienna's foreign policy.[1] However, the leaders of the Russian diplomatic department reacted to the ambass-

[1] Report of Count P. A. Kapnist to the Minister of Foreign Affairs, Count M. N. Murav'ev, dated 12 (NS 24) Feb. 1898. *Arkhiv vneshnei politiki Rossiiskoi imperii Ministerstva inostrannykh del Rossii* (hereafter AVPRI), *fond* 133 (*Kantselyariya*), *opis'* 470, *listy* 32–40 (with versos).

ador's plan with reserve or even coldly. The Russian Minister for Foreign Affairs, Count Mikhail Nikolaevich Murav'ev, though ready to enter an agreement with Austria-Hungary on a particular question, was not willing to look far ahead. Probably for this reason in correspondence with Count Kapnist he refrained from exchanging opinions on this subject. The head of Russian diplomacy in 1900, Count Vladimir Nikolaevich Lambsdorff, displayed greater activity in Balkan affairs, but did not share the opinion of the ambassador in Vienna.

As the movement for national liberation grew among the Sultan's European subjects, Count Kapnist attempted to persuade his superiors to intensify co-operation with Vienna by removing conditions 'which hitherto have inhibited any further development of it [i.e. of the agreement]'.[2] Count Lambsdorff's reply was categorical: the agreement of 1897 was to be regarded as having a 'more or less temporary nature' and 'having been of material value to the cause of pacifying the Balkan nationalities'; therefore, there was no sense in 'continuing the exchange of opinions in every particular case, for one can state in advance that, in view of the opposing aims of Russia and Austria-Hungary, discussions of particular questions are hardly likely to lead to practical results'.[3] Count Kapnist was thus in fact forbidden to take practical steps to extend bilateral relations. The only steps proposed were those protecting the Balkan peninsula from convulsions of any kind.

However, the Sultan's European possessions in the first years of the twentieth century were on the brink of rebellion. It was clear to the Great Powers, above all to Russia and Austria-Hungary, that the mere maintenance of the principle of the status quo was no longer sufficient and was not, in fact, a possible option. The pacification of the Ottoman provinces of south-east Europe could be attained only by means of changes in the Turkish administration. For this it was necessary to persuade the Sultan to accept the necessity of reform and to agree with the Great Powers a mode of action in the Balkan peninsula. For Russia and Austria-Hungary this was an appropriate occasion to show initiative, based on the experience of previous co-operation. There thus arose a need for further development of the 1897 agreement or for its replacement by a new document. The exchange of opinions between St Petersburg and Vienna, and the co-ordination of their positions with each other and with the Great Powers, were accompanied by a conflict

[2] Report of Count P. A. Kapnist to Count V. N. Lambsdorff, dated 3 (NS 15) Jan. 1899. Ibid., *delo* 107, *list* 14–14 *ob*.

[3] Draft for a secret letter from Count V. N. Lambsdorff to Count P. A. Kapnist. AVPRI, *fond* 151 (*politicheskii arkhiv*), *opis'* 482, *delo* 54, *listy* 4–6 *ob*. Note of Tsar Nicholas II: 'Otlichnyi otvet. Petergof, 3 iyunya 1901.'

of views. Nevertheless, on 3 October (OS 29 September) 1903 in Mürzsteg during a meeting between Tsar Nicholas II and the Emperor Francis Joseph their ministers for foreign affairs, Count Lambsdorff and Count Agenor Gołuchowski, signed an agreement on a plan for reform in the three Turkish vilayets constituting Macedonia, namely Monastir, Kosovo, and Salonica.

Drawn up in the form of instructions to the ambassadors of Russia and Austria-Hungary in Constantinople, the Mürzsteg Programme envisaged significant reforms in the Macedonian vilayets under the surveillance and with the direct participation of Russia and Austria-Hungary. Shared control of Macedonia was established, and the claims to Macedonia of the independent Balkan states were jointly held in check. The declared co-operation of St Petersburg and Vienna did not eliminate the roots of their struggle for influence in the Balkan capitals. But, thanks to the agreement, their rivalry relaxed somewhat and entered into a definite framework, whose boundaries were not to be transgressed. There was a restraint on the political aspirations and actions of the two Great Powers which could operate until the formal abrogation of the agreement. Meanwhile, having been concluded when Europe was virtually divided into two military and political blocs (the Triple Alliance was already an accomplished fact and the Triple Entente was imminent), the Mürzsteg Programme provoked an ambiguous reaction among Russian diplomats and in the central apparatus of the Ministry of Foreign Affairs. Consequently, the heads of the diplomatic department in St Petersburg wished to compile a prognosis of the possible development of events in the Balkan peninsula.

The document published in the Appendix below[4] contains an exposition and analysis of the most coherently formed opinions among Russian diplomats on the fate of the European vilayets of the Porte in connection with their reformation under the aegis of Russia and Austria-Hungary. They were expressed at the instigation of Count Lambsdorff by the full privy councillors[5] Aleksandr Ivanovich Nelidov and Ivan Alekseevich Zinov'ev, Russian ambassadors to France and Turkey respectively and acknowledged experts on the eastern question and Balkan upheavals. Their opinions were analysed and furnished with his own opinions by Count Kapnist. All three of these highly placed men were agreed on the inevitability of change in Turkey's European domains. However, they had varying views on ways of bringing change about and on the limits of acceptable reform.

Nelidov put forward a plan of reform which obviously was not workable, based on a final solution of the eastern question 'by our firm

[4] Ibid, *listy* 57–73.

[5] *Deistvitel'nyi tainyi sovetnik* was the highest civil rank and second in the Table of Ranks.

establishment on the Bosporus, with the *opening of the Dardanelles* and a protectorate over Constantinople, the Turkish capital, or a *free city*'.[6] As consequences of this Nelidov envisaged the creation, on the basis of Article 23 of the Treaty of Berlin, of an autonomous Macedonia, and the reformation of the Adrianople vilayet, from which the hinterland in the area of the straits would be estranged to Russia's advantage. The whole plan was based on favouring Bulgaria in her ambition to unite with Macedonia, as a result of which she should not oppose the Russian presence in the straits.[7] In reality, Nelidov was putting forward another of his plans for Russia to gain control of the Black Sea straits. He was a proponent of the partition of the Ottoman Empire and the Straits were an obsession which had caused him professional embarrassment: in 1896, after advancing this risky project, he had, at the Sultan's request, been recalled from his post as ambassador in Constantinople.

Zinov'ev considered the question of reforms exclusively from the viewpoint of their 'practical attainability' in the interests of Russia.[8] He therefore proposed that the Balkan states be given no ground for opening the eastern question. By this he understood refusing to define the ethnic boundaries in the Macedonian vilayets, since this might lead to complications among the nationalities; not permitting the formation in the Balkan Peninsula of a strong state (meaning Bulgaria); and, if possible, restricting the area of reform to the Kosovo, Monastir, and Salonika vilayets. He excluded the Adrianople vilayet from the programme of reform, provided that reforms to improve the position of Christians were implemented there by the Turkish government.[9] Zinov'ev considered that a fundamental reform of the European provinces of Turkey should not begin until Russia had enjoyed all the advantage it had a right to expect. Before that all efforts should be directed towards realizing the Mürzsteg Programme.[10] These, in general terms, were the views of the Russian ambassador to Turkey on the present and future of the European vilayets of the Ottoman Empire. Both ambassadors saw the development and resolution of the Balkan question in terms of military intervention by the Great Powers and the severance from Turkey of her European provinces with the inevitable performance by Russsia of her 'historical task'. It is quite clear that their thoughts did not correspond to the political realities of Russia at the beginning of the twentieth century. Such ideas, especially those of Nelidov, were not capable of acceptance even as a working hypothesis.

Thus Count Kapnist was given a perfect opportunity to put before the heads of the Ministry of Foreign Affairs his own view of the future of

[6] AVPRI, *fond* 151, *opis'* 482, *delo* 54, *list* 58. [7] Ibid., *list* 57–57 *ob*.

[8] Ibid., *list* 59. [9] Ibid. [10] Ibid.

the Balkan problems. Emphasizing that at present the only possible subject for discussion was the realization of the programme of reforms agreed at Mürzsteg, he expressed his opinion of 'what should be borne in mind and where it should lead'.[11] He presented a plan for the peaceful settlement of the fate of the Macedonian vilayets under the aegis of the Great Powers, principally of Russia and Austria-Hungary. He suggested using the precedents of Eastern Rumelia and Crete by taking the Monastir, Kosovo, and Salonika vilayets under international control. This step need not mean the beginning of the dissolution of the Ottoman Empire. On the contrary, it would temporarily strengthen it by freeing it of territories causing it anxiety.[12] The mechanism for realizing the plan consisted of an agreement between Russia and Austria-Hungary supported by other European states.[13] This would be the embodiment of the co-operation between Russia and Austria-Hungary which had been approved in the preparation for the Mürzteg Programme and of which he [Kapnist] had been an ardent adherent. In the final analysis Count Kapnist recognized as necessary the partition of the three provisionally reformed and pacified Macedonian vilayets between the interested Balkan states. This would unite them 'under the protection of Orthodox Russia' and would facilitate the completion by Russia of its 'liberating, historical' task in the Near East. Only after this would Russia be able to 'devote herself to the settlement of another task, essential to her own interests [. . .], the question of the Straits'.[14] Kapnist did not indicate a time for the fulfilment of his plan. However, he emphasized that haste in the proposed transformations would be inadmissible.

Such were the reflections of three highly placed Russian diplomats on the future of the Turkish provinces with Christian populations. They saw that the systems of administration there were condemned, and understood the necessity of solving the questions of national self-determination of the peoples living in the Balkan peninsula. Of the three the most mature and elegant plan is Kapnist's. Its deficiency, however, from the point of view of the general direction of Russia's foreign policy was the aspiration to rely on the co-operation of Russia and Austria-Hungary, which he was inclined to interpret broadly, and on the benevolence of the Concert of Europe, which no longer existed.

The document, which is typed, is neither dated nor signed, but Kapnist's authorship and the time of writing (the end of September or the beginning of October (OS) 1903) can be established from the contents. The spelling has been modernized. An oblique stroke in red pencil at the beginning of the document is proof that it was read by Tsar Nicholas II. Words underlined by the author are printed in italic.

[11] Ibid., *list* 63. [12] Ibid., *list* 66.
[13] Ibid. [14] Ibid., *listy* 68 *ob.*–69 *ob.*

APPENDIX

Document on the Future of Turkey's European Possessions

л. 57 В доверительных письмах от апреля и мая месяцев сего года императорские послы в Париже и Константинополе, по предложению министра иностранных дел, изложили свои соображения относительно способов разрешения вопросов, касающихся Балканского полуострова.

Исходя с различных точек зрения, Д. Т. С. Нелидов и Д. Т. С. Зиновьев пришли к тому заключению, что в случае необходимости дальнейшего шага на пути постепенного изъятия македонских вилаетов из под турецкого владычества, предпочтительно было бы остановиться на образовании одной целокупной автономии для трех вилаетов — Монастырского, Коссовского и Салоникского, составляющих ту разношерстную область, которую привыкли называть Македонией; а не пытаться разделить эту область на отдельные автономные единицы, либо на основании существующих очертаний вилаетов, либо на основании более соответствующего этнографического разверстания.

Сходясь в таком заключении, оба посла, впрочем, совершенно расходятся в доводах и соображениях, которые их к нему приводят.

Д. Т. С. Нелидов усматривает в создании целокупной автономной ‖
л. 57 об. Македонии зародыш будущего независимого Македонского княжества, правительство которого не стремилось бы к присоединению ни к Болгарии, ни к Сербии, ни к Греции, и каковое княжество, получив свободный доступ к морю, имело бы все условия независимого существования. Первоначальный устав такой автономной Македонии мог бы быть выработан на основании статьи 23 Берлинского трактата. Соседние маленькие балканские государства не имели бы никакого серьезного основания быть недовольными созданием нового Балканского княжества, так как законные их требования были бы удовлетворены тем, что соплеменные населения были бы поставлены в улучшенные самостоятельные условия существования.

Затем, по мнению Д. Т. С. Нелидова, следовало бы предоставить времени решить, в каком направлении развитие подвинется далее и каким образом, следовательно, произойдет окончательное решение Балканского вопроса.

Не упоминая прямым образом о вероятии слияния, в более или менее близком будущем, автономной Македонии с Болгарией, Д. Т. С. Нелидов косвенно, тем не менее, касается такого события, находя совершенно естественным стремление Болгарского княжества к объединению с соплеменным населением, составляющим большинство христиан македонских вилаетов; такое стремление, по мнению Д. Т. С. Нелидова тем
л. 58 более ‖ было бы естественно, что вследствии начертания для Болгарии С. Стефанским трактатом широких границ, со всех концов Македонии стали стекаться в Княжество для науки и службы молодые славяне, пользующиеся ныне приобретенным положением, чтобы способствовать освобождению своих братьев, оставшихся под турецким игом.

Д. Т. С. Нелидов идет далее, утверждая, что было бы несправедливо оставить на произвол турок Адрианопольский вилает; что ни один здравомыслящий болгарин не станет помышлять о наследии оттоманского владычества на проливах и что, следовательно, болгарский гинтерланд, прилегающий к Босфору и Дарданеллам был бы благоприятнее для нашего обладания, чем греческий, в виду неблагодарности к нему греческого народа. По словам Д. Т. С. Нелидова, наибольшая часть македонских славян подходит к болгарам, а не к сербам; греки же сплошною массою населяют лишь прибрежье. Поэтому Д. Т. С. Нелидов признает, что болгарский ирредентизм, делающий столь громадные успехи на политико-религиозной почве в борьбе против Константинопольской патриархии, соответствует интересам не только Болгарии, но и России.

В заключении своего письма Д. Т. С. Нелидов указывает на разрешение восточного вопроса через прочное утверждение наше на Босфоре, с *открытием Дарданелл* и протекторатом над Константинополем — турецкою столицею или *вольным городом*. ‖

Склоняясь в пользу установления единой целостной автономии для всей л. 58 об.
Македонии, преимущественно перед раздроблением этой области на три отдельные автономные единицы, Д. Т. С. Зиновьев рассуждает совершенно иначе.

Он, повидимому, не разделяет иллюзий ни относительно образования прочного самостоятельного государства из Македонии, ни относительно удовлетворения таким способом вожделений соседних маленьких балканских государств.

Становясь на чисто практическую почву Д. Т. С. Зиновьев склоняется в принципе в пользу назначения одного христианского губернатора для всей Македонии лишь по следующим соображениям, а именно: потому что настоящее деление Македонии на три вилаета совершенно произвольно и не отвечает этнографическим границам; потому что преждевременное определение частей Турции, которые должны отойти каждому из балканских государств, было бы для них поощрением, которое повлекло бы за собою открытие восточного вопроса; и, наконец, потому что, в случае образования трех отдельных автономных единиц, каждая из них оказалась бы слишком слабою, чтобы устоять против происков соседей.

Затем Д. Т. С. Зиновьев не закрывает глаза на трудность и неудобства образования единой автономной Македонии и приходит к заключению, что оно не было бы возможным без прямого военного вмешательства со стороны европейских Великих держав. ‖

Одним словом, императорский посол в Константинополе обсуждает л. 59
вопрос исключительно с точки зрения большей или меньшей практической удобоисполнимости, в данный момент, того или другого проекта для Македонии.

С общей точки зрения он высказывается лишь в том смысле, что образование на Балканском полуострове слишком сильного государства (подразумевается, конечно, Болгария) не было бы желательно для наших интересов и что в случае образования автономной Македонии, Адрианопольский вилает должен быть обеспечен за Турцией, но под условием, однако, чтобы оттоманское правительство обязалось ввести в нем реформы в пользу христиан.

В заключении своего письма Д. Т. С. Зиновьев высказывает мнение, что к переустройству Балканского полуострова желательно было бы приступить не ранее того времени, когда императорское правительство было бы в состоянии воспользоваться всеми выгодами, на которые оно в праве рассчитывать; а также, что пока не наступит потребность в изменении нашей настоящей программы реформ, все усилия должны быть направлены исключительно к осуществлению этой программы.

Автор настоящей записки позволяет себе сделать нижеследующие замечания относительно мнений, высказанных императорскими послами в Париже и Константинополе. ‖

л. 59 об. Что касается соображений Д. Т. С. Нелидова, составитель записки никак не может, в принципе, разделить иллюзии относительно возможности образовать из этнографически разношерстной Македонии, окруженной соплеменными государствами, какое-то срединное Македонское княжество. Он не разделяет иллюзий и относительно удовлетворения таким путем вожделений соседних государств посредством улучшения условий существования их соплеменников — это равносильно было бы признанию, что соседние маленькие государства руководствуются исключительно гуманитарными стремлениями (часто выставляемыми ими вперед), а не весьма определенными национальными и государственными стремлениями. Автор записки не разделяет и веру Д. Т. С. Нелидова в то, «что ни один здравомыслящий болгарин не мечтает о наследии Турции на Босфор» и что любовь Болгарии к России служит достаточным залогом против соперничества с нами на этой почве. Автору записки не хотелось бы поручиться в этом отношении ни за последователей идеи «Великой Болгарии», ни за болгарских политических деятелей, ни за князя Фердинанда. Затем дело идет не только о настоящем, но и о будущем.

По мнению его, целокупная автономная Македония, в противоположность того, что предполагает Д. Т. С. Нелидов, неминуемо сделалась бы гнездом для интриг и тайной борьбы между соседними маленькими государствами, а может быть и театром соревнования между Великими державами. ‖

л. 60 Неопределенность будущего развития и предоставление на произвол случайностей окончательного разрешения Балканского вопроса, как это явствовало бы из соображений Д. Т. С. Нелидова, также никаким образом не может быть признано желательным. Такой образ действия служил бы лишь продолжением той бессознательной и лишенной ясной конечной цели политики, которой именно предполагается положить предел.

Д. Т. С. Нелидов требует, как и балканские правительства и балканские политические агитаторы, применения к Македонии 23 статьи Берлинского трактата, с той, однако, разницей, что последние видят в таком применении вероятное начало общей смуты и предлог к удовлетворению своих вожделений; между тем, как Д. Т. С. Нелидов видит в применении реформ, выработанных европейской комиссией панацею для образования какой-то идеальной Македонии-Аркадии, с широким самоуправлением, на основании выборного народного представительства и с местными административными советами, которые постепенно выработали бы распределение по народностям (?). Такое воображаемое этнографически-разношерстное, но обладающее широким самоуправлением государство, никак не могло бы, впрочем, согласоваться с теми данными, которые приводятся в начале письма Д. Т. С. Нелидова, относительно подавляющего большинства болгарского элемента в Македонии и совершенной основательности ‖ болгарского ирредентизма в этой области. л. 60 об.

При всем этом, еще не нужно терять из виду совершенно справедливое замечание императорского посла в Константинополе, что, в случае образования единой Македонии под управлением единого христианского губернатора, с применением к ней автономного управления на основании Берлинского трактата, неминуемо возник бы вопрос о том, как удалить из нее турецкие войска и какой военной силе поручить после того ограждение и поддержание порядка в столь неестественно сплоченной воедино области. На такой вопрос Д. Т. С. Зиновьев отвечает указанием на неизбежность прибегнуть к общеевропейской оккупации. Невольно приходит на мысль в этих обстоятельствах вопрос о том, какие были бы последствия такой оккупации, в особенности при наличности полной неопределенности конечного способа разрешения Балканского вопроса, предоставляемого, по соображениям Д. Т. С. Нелидова, на произвол будущих случайностей. Нынешние затруднения и пререкания, возникшие вследствии простой посылки известного числа европейских офицеров для образования жандармерии, казалось бы могли бы дать предчувствовать ответ на вопрос, что произошло бы в Македонии в случае общей европейской оккупации.

Следует еще отметить в письме Д. Т. С. Нелидова нескрываемое пристрастие к болгарским вожделениям не только в ущерб греческим, но и сербским. Допущение участия Греции в какой-либо мере в наследии ‖ турецкому владычеству в Македонии, он считает невозможным вследствие л. 61
явной неблагодарности эллинского народа к нам. Касательно же Сербии и Черногории Д. Т. С. Нелидов предполагает, что устройство единой и независимой Македонии и не должно бы вызвать с их стороны противодействий. Между тем, весьма положительные данные доказывают, что Сербия и Черногория самым энергичным образом высказываются именно против такого объединения Македонии, усматривая в нем простой этап к аннексированию со стороны Болгарии.

Нельзя вообще не отметить, что все упомянутые соображения носят на себе отпечаток сентиментальной политики, основанной скорее на всеславянских мечтаниях и увлечениях, чем на холодной и здравой оценке интересов с русской государственной точки зрения. Заключения, основанные, например, на «неблагодарности» греков и на «любви» к нам славянских элементов, свидетельствуют о таком направлении, упускающем из вида, что «чувства» не составляют в политике надежной основы, а также что без уравновешенного удовлетворения по возможности всем интересам, немыслима устойчивость, составляющая необходимое условие для правильного решения политических вопросов.

Нельзя, наконец, не обратить внимания на набросанный в конце письма Д. Т. С. Нелидова, в общих чертах, способ разрешения восточного вопроса вообще посредством утверждения нашего протектората над Кон-‖
стантинополем, но с *открытием Дарданелл* и обращением *Стамбула в* л. 61 об.
вольный город. Под открытием Дарданелл очевидно подразумевается свободный пропуск через этот пролив военных судов всех наций, так как

свободный проход торговых судов обеспечен уже теперь. Объявление же Константинополя вольным городом должно считаться равносильным его нейтрализации. Спрашивается, чем было бы обеспечено со стороны суши и со стороны моря, в случае осуществления такой комбинации, закрытие Черного моря для европейских военных судов закрытие, составляющее не только наше право, но и существенное условие обороны на случай войны?

Впрочем об этом следует упомянуть лишь мимоходом, так как разрешение балканского вопроса и разрешение восточного вопроса во всей своей совокупности составляют два совершенно отдельных предмета, которые, при правильном ходе дел, должны разрешаться поочередно одни после другого, а отнюдь не одновременно.

Из всего вышесказанного видно, что противоположность в мнениях между маститым дипломатом, представляющим Россию в Париже, и автором записки, противоположность коренная, так как она проистекает от совершенного различия в политических воззрениях.

Различие в соображениях императорского посла в Константинополе и
л. 62 составителя записки — совершенно другого рода. ‖ Оно основано отчасти на некоторых недоразумениях и отчасти на разнице в точке зрения относительно предложенного министром иностранных дел вопроса. Существует, конечно, и совершенная противоположность мнений, но это лишь по некоторым частным вопросам.

Прежде всего составитель настоящей записки согласен с мнением Д. Т. С. Зиновьева, что пока не наступит потребность в изменении нашей программы, все усилия должны быть направлены к осуществлению намеченных в Мюрцштеге реформ и к удержанию балканских государств от попыток, способных нарушить наступившее на Балканском полуострове сравнительное спокойствие и помешать улучшениям.

Он совершенно согласен и с тем, что в виду настоящего положения дел на Балканском полуострове, не представляется причин, которые побуждали бы нас желать изменения этого положения.

По вопросу о том, когда именно наступит потребность в изменении и насколько настоящее положение является прочным, мнение многоопытного посла в Константинополе должно иметь решающее значение.

Относительно желательности того, чтобы приступлено было к переустройству Балканского полуострова не ранее того времени, когда императорское правительство будет в состоянии воспользоваться выгодами,
л. 62 об. на которые оно имеет право, также не может быть разногласия. ‖ Насколько же это будет возможно, зависит от обстоятельств, оценка коих принадлежит также исключительно авторитетному наблюдателю на месте, столь близко знакомому со всеми балканскими делами.

Риск преждевременного открытия всего восточного вопроса через поспешный и необдуманный шаг в балканских делах, никогда не входил в соображения автора записки.

Напротив того, по его мнению правильное, постепенное и осторожное разрешение Балканского вопроса, никогда не делая, так сказать, шага вперед иначе как под гнетом необходимости, составляет лучший способ для отсрочки, на возможно отдаленное время, поднятия всего восточного вопроса во всем его объеме.

Но для такого правильного и своевременного переустройства на Балканском полуострове первым условием является, по убеждению автора записки, установление конечной цели такого устойчивого и сообразного с интересами России переустройства. Такое установление конечной цели служило бы руководящей нитью для совокупного и согласного действия всех органов русского правительства, причастных к этому делу на всех ступенях дипломатической иерархии.

Конечно, определить вперед точно и подробно полную программу с опеделенными сроками для каждого этапа, было бы невозможно, так как необходимо считаться с обстоятельствами и с живыми факторами, участвующими в деле. Но конечная желательная цель должна быть ‖ выяснена вперед и разногласия относительно нее не должно существовать. л. 63

Одним словом вопрос заключается не в том, что должно быть *предпринято сейчас*, этот вопрос уже был разрешен в Мюрцштеге, а в том, что следует *иметь в виду и к чему вести?*

В этом именно отношении, повидимому, произошло недоразумение между Д. Т. С. Зиновьевым и автором этой записки, так как ими обсуждался вопрос, поставленный министром иностранных дел, в двух разных смыслах.

Переходя затем к рассмотрению причин, побуждающих Д. Т. С. Зиновьева дать преимущество назначению державами одного христианского генерал-губернатора для всей автономной Македонии перед раздроблением этой области на три отдельные автономии, следует заметить, что все эти причины практического свойства и что они касаются большей удобоприменимости, в данную минуту, одной системы сравнительно с другой.

A) Прежде всего Д. Т. С. Зиновьев обращает внимание на то, что границы трех Македонских вилаетов совершенно произвольны и не отвечают этнографии и, что вследствии этого, назначение трех губернаторов, принадлежащх к трем христианским национальностям, имело бы большие неудобства.

И в этом отношении кроется, по всем вероятиям, недоразумение. ‖

Предлагая назначение трех губернаторов, как запасную, так сказать, меру л. 63 об. для того момента, когда применение Мюрцштегских реформ оказалось бы уже недостаточным, и дальнейший шаг на пути эмансипации христианского народонаселения стал бы неизбежным, автор настоящей записки отнюдь не выставлял эту меру как единственно возможную для подготовки окончательного разрешения в предполагаемом им смысле балканского вопроса.

Ему весьма хорошо была известна не только произвольность существующего разграничения трех вилаетов, но еще умышленная со стороны Турции его несообразность, хотя он и не обладал, как Д. Т. С. Зиновьев, достаточными статистическими и этнографическими сведениями по этому предмету.

Но такая неправильность в разграничении вилаетов, по мнению автора записки, не была бы достаточною причиною, чтобы исключить, в принципе, разверстание македонской области на три большие, хотя и разной величины, участка, в которых не только преобладала бы та или другая национальность, но которые еще отвечали бы и другим условиям, необходимым для окончательного разрешения Балканского вопроса.

Такое разверстание автор записки не считает невозможным в принципе, хотя оно и было бы сопряжено с некоторыми этнографическими неудобствами.

Назначение трех губернаторов, принадлежащих трем национальностям, ‖
л. 64 автор записки рекомендовал лишь как подготовительную меру к разделу Македонии, на случай невозможности дальнейшей отсрочки разрешения Балканского вопроса, и на случай недостатка времени предварительно настоять на столь необходимом, во многих отношениях, перегранилении вилаетов.

Такое мнение его было высказано несколько месяцев тому назад в тот момент, когда еще мирное применение Мюрцштегской программы казалось довольно сомнительным и когда, повидимому, балканские государства, в особенности Болгария, готовились к серьезной борьбе в нынешнее лето. Ежели события, совершенно независимые от балканских дел, с тех пор косвенно повлияли на положение дел в Балканском полуострове, то в то время предвидеть это было довольно трудно и, во всяком случае, отсрочка кризиса не избавляет от необходимости выяснить и наметить конечную цель.

Ежели могут быть придуманы деятелями более знакомыми с местными условиями меры более удобные для подготовления того конечного результата, к которому следует вести дело, то автор записки первый готов к ним присоединиться.

Он не сомневается, что ежели только существующее устройство Македонии, улучшенное применением Мюрцштегских реформ, могло бы только продержаться некоторое время, то не было бы никакой надобности прибегать к непосредственному назначению трех христианских
л. 64 об. губернаторов в вилаеты при теперешнем их разграничении, а гораздо ‖ более было бы целесообразно первоначально настоять на перегранилении этих вилаетов.

Такое перегранилчение было бы уже необходимо и по отношению к Албании, так как, при определении существующих границ, Порта умышленно руководствовалась желанием как можно более перемешать национальности и, в особенности втиснуть албанский элемент в Коссовский и Монастырский вилаеты.

Может быть перегранилчение оказалось бы необходимым до некоторой степени и по отношению к Адрианопольскому вилаету.

Таким образом, могли бы быть исподволь и одновременно подготовлены и точные границы Македонии и окончательный ее раздел.

Затем зависело бы от обстоятельств, пришлось ли бы прямо приступить, когда наступил бы на то неизбежный момент, к такому разделу, или же необходимо было бы предварительно прибегнуть к переходному этапу трех губернаторов, номинально подчиненных Турции.

Б) Второе возражение Д. Т. С. Зиновьева против назначения отдельных христианских губорнаторов в каждый из македонских вилаетов заключается в том, что эта мера послужила бы поощрением вожделениям соседних государств и ускорила бы распадение Турции, что вовсе не было бы желательно в виду крупных осложнений, которое могло бы повлечь за собой открытие Восточного вопроса.

На это можно ответить, что одновременно с назначением трех ‖ христианских губернаторов, принадлежащих к трем национальностям, л. 65 можно было бы первоначально, в виду смягчения этой меры, оставить общий надзор над вилаетами турецкому генеральному инспектору, назначаемому Султаном с согласия Держав, наподобие Хильми-Паши. Во всяком случае, это было бы предпочтительнее назначению единого христианского генерал-губернатора. Упразднение Турецкого владычества над Македонскими вилаетами могло бы произойти, таким образом, совершенно постепенно и без потрясений. *Окончательное же освобождение этих вилаетов от турецкого владычества отнюдь не привело бы, по мнению автора записки, к совершенному расчленению Оттоманской империи, а напротив того, временно могло бы придать ей новую жизненную силу. Освобожденная от постоянной борьбы с усиливающимся христианским населением в Македонии и от чрезмерных расходов для содержания войска в этой области, Турция могла бы сосредоточить все свои силы в остающемся за ней европейском вилаете, прилегающем к проливам и обеспечить на продолжительное время свое положение в Босфоре и в Дарданеллах. Таким образом, утрата Турцией трех вилаетов повлекла бы за собою не открытие восточного вопроса, а напротив того, его отсрочку*.

В) Третье рассуждение, приводимое Д. Т. С. Зиновьевым в пользу предпочтительности единой автономии для всей Македонии, заключается в том, что в противном случае, каждая из отдельных трех автономных ‖ единиц л. 65 об. оказалась бы слишком слабою, чтобы устоять против происков соседей и других неблагоприятных обстоятельств.

Затрудняясь объяснить себе, в чем именно могли бы состоять такие «другие неблагоприятные обстоятельства», можно однако ответить, что единой автономной Македонии, вероятно, еще труднее было бы устоять против болгарских происков, которые притом не преминули бы возбудить ожесточенное противодействие со стороны других соседних государств. При разделении же Македонии на три отдельные автономные единицы, этим самым были бы, так сказать, урегулированы происки каждого из трех соседей и подготовлено естественное нормальное и устойчивое разрешение восточного вопроса.

Не нужно при этом терять из виду, что окончательное отчуждение от Турции трех македонских вилаетов и раздел их между соседними Балканскими государствами составили бы нарушение Берлинского договора и, следовательно, требовали бы соответствующего соглашения между Великими державами, подписавшими договор. Едва ли можно было бы предвидеть, чтобы которая либо из них серьезно противилась подобному разрешению Балканского вопроса. С гораздо большим вероятием можно было бы рассчитывать в этом случае на поддержку всей Европы и ее общественного мнения. Прецеденты Восточной Румелии и Крита позволяют даже надеяться на совершенно мирное течение помянутого переворота. Между тем, авторитет европейского концерта мог бы, в данном случае, оказать свою пользу: перед ним должны были бы ‖ преклониться маленькие л. 66 балканские государства и разграничение установленное европейским договором, заставило бы замолкнуть пререкания между ними.

Перечислив свои возражения против раздела Македонии на отдельные автономные единицы, Д. Т. С. Зиновьев указывает в своем письме неудобства и трудности, сопряженные и с образованием единой автономной области.

Между такими неудобствами и затруднениями первое место занимает то обстоятельство, что он признает оккупацию войсками великих держав совершенно неизбежным условием, хотя бы и не вполне отвечающим нашим видам.

На это нужно заметить, что допущение общеевропейской оккупации было бы возвращением к приему, неоднократно оказавшемуся несостоятельным на почве общеевропейских конференций.

Более целесообразным казалось бы применение, в данном случае, того метода, который уже увенчался некоторым успехом в деле установления программы и применения теперешних реформ.

На первых порах и этот метод считался неприменимым без употребления материальной силы. Между тем, до сих пор без нее обошлось.

Метод состоит в основном соглашении между двумя наиболее заинтересованными державами, в привлечении, затем, остальных европейских держав к поддержке определенной условленной программы и в совокупном давлении, производимом на Порту двумя наиболее
л. 66 об. заинтересованными ‖ державами с поддержкою Европы.

Может быть, что умелое применение такого метода могло бы избавить и в данном случае от неудобств и последствий общеевропейской оккупации.

В заключение своего письма императорский посол в Константинополе признает нежелательным, с точки зрения интересов России, образование на Балканском полуострове слишком сильного государства. Он соглашается с тем, что в случае образования автономной Македонии, Адрианопольский вилает должен был бы быть обеспечен за Турцией; но он прибавляет, что должно быть поставлено в таком случае условие, чтобы Оттоманское правительство обязалось ввести в Адрианопольский вилает все те реформы, которые необходимы для обеспечения интересов христианского населения.

В постановке такого условия заключается единственная, но коренная противоположность мнений между Д. Т. С. Зиновьевым и автором настоящей записки.

Как-то не верится, чтобы тот самый посол, который так часто и наглядно выставлял несовместимость реформ с самою сущностью турецкого управления и доказывал, что применение преобразований равносильно постепенному упразднению турецкого владычества, ныне требовал бы для области, укрепление коей за Турцией считается необходимым, «всех тех реформ, которые нужны для обеспечения интересов христианского населения». ‖

л. 67 Автор настоящей записки самым категорическим образом высказывается против применения каких бы то ни было реформ в Адрианопольском вилаете и в пользу оставления в нем во всей его неприкосновенности турецкого управления, в том убеждении, что всякое введение реформ влечет за собою как европейское вмешательство под тем или другим видом, так и развитие ирредентизма того или другого из соседних государств. Между тем, по убеждению автора записки, Адрианопольский вилает должен быть неприкосновенною территорией, служащей, так сказать, «охраною проливов», территорией, которая должна оставаться под исключительным владычеством Турции до тех пор, пока оно не будет заменено исключительным владычеством России.

Допустимо, с этой точки зрения, лишь некоторое изменение, в случае надобности, в очертании границ вилаета, в видах выселения за такую новую черту всего болгарского элемента, составляющего, впрочем, незначительное меньшинство.

II.

Сделав свои замечания по поводу соображений, представленных императорскими послами в Париже и Константинополе, составитель настоящей записки считает долгом изложить общие основы той политики, которой, по его мнению, следовало бы придерживаться по отношению к ‖ делам Балканского полуострова. л. 67 об.

На этой почве, как и в большей части политических вопросов, можно придерживаться двух разных образов действия: либо неопределенного и, так сказать, бессознательного, предоставляющего случайностям давать то или другое направление; либо образа действия определенного и сознательного, первым условием которого является ясное представление желаемого разрешения вопроса и, затем, строгая и последовательная гармонизация всех мероприятий к достижению намеченной цели.

В данном случае, а именно по отношению к балканским делам, автор записки является убежденным сторонником второй из вышеотмеченных систем.

По его мнению, прежде всего следовало бы сделать себе ясное представление желательного разрешения Балканского вопроса. Но при этом он отнюдь не является сторонником каких бы то ни было преждевременных мероприятий, а напротив того, полагает, что первым условием мирного разрешения было бы последовательное, но постепенное движение вперед к намеченной цели, соображаясь с обстоятельствами и не делая ни одного шага иначе, как под давлением необходимости.

В Мюрцштегской программе реформ, автор записки видит не окончательное разрешение Балканского вопроса, а лишь этап на пути к такому разрешению; но он полагает, вместе с тем, что само собою разумеется, чем более продолжительна была бы остановка на этом этапе, как и на всяком другом, тем было бы лучше. ‖

В тот же момент, когда применение Мюрцштегской программы реформ л. 68 оказалось бы либо невозможным, либо недостаточным, представится выбор между двумя противоположными направлениями и двумя способами разрешения Балканского вопроса, а именно между образованием целокупной автономии для всей Македонской области и разделом Македонии на три отдельные автономные единицы, сперва может быть на основании существующего административного деления, но конечно с целью приспособления, впоследствии такого деления, по мере возможности, к этнографическим условиям.

Отдавая себе отчет в последствиях выбора между тем и другим

мероприятием, автор записки высказывается категорически в пользу второй системы, так как она вела бы к тому разрешению Балканского вопроса, который он считает единственным правильным и устойчивым.

Прежде чем приступить к изложению своих воззрений по этому предмету, он считает необходимым оговориться в том смысле, что Балканский вопрос является, в его глазах, лишь составной частью так называемого ближневосточного вопроса. Разрешение первого не должно необходимо влечь за собою открытие второго. Напротив того, при мирном и нормальном ходе дела, разрешение первой части вопроса, т.е. переустройство на Балканском полуострове, должно бы предшествовать открытию и разрешению ближневосточного вопроса во всем его объеме.

л. 68 об. Об этом последнем ныне, может быть, еще рано говорить, хотя и ‖ его не следует терять из виду.

Необходимость же дальнейшего шага на пути разрешения балканского вопроса, может представиться со дня на день, и потому было бы совершенно своевременным ясно представить себе, что именно следует иметь в виду и к чему вести?

Составитель записки делает себе следующее представление о разрешении балканского вопроса:

Точное очертание сферы применения, как настоящих, так и будущих реформ, т.е. трех македонских вилаетов с надлежащею ректификациею их границ, главным образом со стороны Албании, а может быть, и со стороны Адрианопольского вилаета.

Вперед подготовленный раздел между тремя соседними балканскими государствами, Болгарией, Сербией и Грецией, так называемой Македонской области.

Образование автономной Албании, вассальной Турции и обеспеченной от аннексирования какой-либо из великих держав или соседних маленьких государств.

Прочное закрепление за Турцией в нынешнем его составе, или же перерграниченного, Адрианопольского вилаета.

Компромисс между Россией и Австро-Венгрией относительно прав, предоставленных этой последней державе Берлинским трактатом относительно Ново-Базарского санджака.

Таково было бы в общих чертах окончательное разрешение балканского вопроса. ‖

л. 69 Буде эти основные начала были приняты императорским правительством, — осуществление их в более или менее отдаленном будущем должно было бы впредь составлять конечную и ясную цель политики России на почве балканских дел.

Такая раз установленная цель должна бы впредь служить руководящею нитью, как для всех подготовительных мероприятий со стороны императорского правительства, так и для совокупной гармонической деятельности всех его органов, соприкосновенных с балканскими делами.

Вышенамеченное разрешение балканского вопроса имело бы, по мнению автора записки, следующие результаты:

Оно дало бы полное и правильное удовлетворение вожделениям маленьких балканских государств, являющихся естественными наследниками, в определенной сфере, постепенно разлагающегося оттоманского владычества над христианскими племенами.

Такое разрешение балканского вопроса установило бы в центре полуострова уравновешенный и устойчивый строй, служащий залогом будущего спокойствия.

Оно удовлетворило бы также периодически возмущаемому турецкими зверствами европейскому общественному мнению и отняло бы предлог для вмемательства и происков на Балканском полуострове со стороны западных держав.

Вместе с тем, помянутое разрешение балканского вопроса положило бы конец легенде об австро-венгерских вожделениях на Салоники, ‖ *или же* л. 69 об. *пресекло бы возможность всякой попытки в этом направлении, — буде такие вожделения действительно существовали.*

Наконец, что может быть важнее всего другого, правильное и устойчивое разрешение балканского вопроса довершило бы выполнение освободительной исторической задачи России на Ближнем Востоке. Ей надлежало бы затем посвятить себя разрешению другой — существенной для ее собственных интересов — задаче на Ближнем Востоке, а именно вопросу проливов.

Маленьким христианским государствам, поставленным Россией на ноги, назначены были бы окончательные границы и им вверено было бы управление христианского населения, освобожденного Россией от мусульманского ига. Тогда, но только тогда, могла бы быть речь о сближении между этими маленькими государствами под сенью православной России.

Как выше сказано, составитель настоящей записки отнюдь не предусматривает надобности какой-либо поспешности на пути достижения намеченной цели. Напротив того, он считал бы желательным всевозможные замедления и возможно продолжительные остановки на каждом этапе последовательного развития. При этом лишь условии можно было бы надеяться на мирное совершение переворота.

Переустройство на Балканском полуострове, как также выше отмечено, сопряжено было бы с нарушением Берлинского трактата, т.е. существующего status quo и, поэтому, требовало бы соглашения с ‖ другими л. 70 великими державами. Но следовало бы крайне оберегаться доведению такого соглашения до совокупного дипломатического и, тем более, материального вмешательства Европы, о котором упоминается в письме Д. Т. С. Зиновьева.

Надлежащий метод для преобразования на Балканском полуострове найден и, до некоторой степени уже испытан. Целесообразно было бы придерживаться того же метода и при дальнейшем развитии балканского вопроса.

Положительное точное и добросовестное соглашение между двумя наиболее заинтересованными державами должно было бы предшествовать вступлению в окончательный его фазис балканского вопроса.

Что же касается, наконец, способов подготовления выше изложенного в общих чертах переустройства на Балканском полуострове, то автор настоящей записки находит, что изыскание таких способов принадлежит не

столько ему самому, сколько более компетентным в балканских делах деятелям. Он убежден только, что главным условием успеха в достижении результатов, раз окончательная цель была бы ясно намечена и установлена, состояла бы в полной гармонии между всеми даже второстепенными мероприятиями, а также в вполне гармонической деятельности всех даже второстепенных органов правительства. Такой последовательный образ действий исключил бы возможность такого рода явлений, как, например,
л. 70 об. усиленной деятельности того, или другого ‖ консула в пользу болгаро-экзархацкой пропаганды в Салоникском вилаете; либо же содействия того или другого дипломатического представителя в пользу распространения реформ на чисто албанское население или в пределах Адрианопольского вилаета. Подразумевается, конечно, тот случай, когда разрешение балканского вопроса в вышепомянутом смысле признано было бы императорским правительством окончательной целью его политики.

В заключение, автор настоящей записки позволяет себе представить, в виде простого проекта подлежащего обсуждению, краткую программу тех последовательных подготовительных мер, которые могли бы, может быть, по его мнению, привести к правильному разрешению балканского вопроса:

1/ Точное очертание Македонской области, с надлежащим изменением границы Коссовского и Монастырского вилаетов, прилегающей к Албании, а также, может быть, и с изменением границ Адрианопольского вилаета.

2/ Новое разграничение между собой трех македонских вилаетов или же их санджаков, с возможным применением к этнографической группировке.

3/ Как скоро явилась бы необходимость нового шага вперед на пути эмансипации македонских вилаетов от турецкого владычества, — назначение
л. 71 христианских губернаторов, принадлежащих трем главным ‖ балканским племенам, с предоставлением им управления областей, в которых их соплеменники составляют большинство, причем конечно Салоникский вилает должен был бы быть значительно уменьшен.

4/ Для смягчения этой меры такие христианские губернаторы, назначаемые Портой, с согласия держав могли бы быть на некоторое время поставлены под верховный надзор, не общего для всей области христианского генерал-губернатора, а под надзор турецкого главного инспектора, наподобие Хильми-Паши, назначаемого султаном, с согласия держав.

5/ Ежели бы такой опыт с христианскими губернаторами оказался неудачным, как некоторые предсказывают, вследствие недостаточности их авторитета; или же этот опыт через некоторое время привел к неудержимому обоюдному стремлению к слиянию с соседними христианскими государствами, что было бы довольно естественно, то на этом переходном этапе не предстояло бы надобности останавливаться особенно долгое время и надлежало бы перейти к разделу на основании вперед условленного между двумя наиболее заинтересованными державами плана, который затем был бы предложен другим державам, для поддержки с их стороны.

6/ Как скоро раздел был бы признан в принципе конечной целью, надлежало бы посвятить особенное внимание определению той части ‖

Салоникского вилаета, которая ближе прилегает к морю и которая, согласно л. 71 об. с мыслью составителя записки должна бы быть аннексирована к Греции.

Этот географически-этнографический вопрос слишком сложен, чтобы он мог быть исчерпан в рамках этой записки, в которой возможно лишь отметить общие начала такого разграничения и вопросы, с которыми оно стоит в связи.

Аннексирование Салоник к Греции является желательным: во-первых, чтобы дать удовлетворение и греческому элементу рядом со славянскими и, таким образом, обоспечить равновесие, на котором зиждется устойчивость; во-вторых, для того, чтобы столь важный приморский пункт как Салоники не попал в руки ни Болгарии, ни Сербии. Для первой это было бы несоразмерным усилением; для второй — слишком отдаленным пунктом от ее центра, что повело бы к необходимости прирезать к Сербии совершенно чуждые ей территории.

Участок прирезываемый к Греции не должен был бы вдаваться чрезмерно в глубь вилаета и ни в коем случае не распространяться вдоль моря до непосредственной близости с Дарданеллами, оканчиваясь примерно около устья Струмы.

Вопрос большего или меньшего протяжения греческого участка, впрочем, стоит в зависимости от разрешения другого вопроса, а именно: что было бы предпочтительнее с точки зрения интересов России, Болгария ли, замкнутая в Черном море и, следовательно, легче ‖ контролируемая? Или же Болгария, л. 72 сидяшая на двух морях — Черном и Эгейском и замыкающая со стороны земли территорию, прилегающую к проливам?

Большее или меньшее протяжение побережья, предназначаемого Греции и большее или меньшее протяжение территории, оставляемой за Турцией, должны бы зависеть от разрешения этого вопроса.

Автор этой записки высказывает, только по этому предмету то убеждение, что при разрешение помянутых вопросов не следовало бы руководствоваться соображениями сентиментального характера, как например: «неблагодарность» к России эллинов, или «любовь» к России болгар, а соображениями, основанными на устойчивости нового строя и на государственных интересах России по отношению к проливам.

Раз решено было бы предоставить, при разделе Македонии, известный участок Салониского вилаета Греции, само собой разумеется это должно было бы иметь непременным последствием противодействие с нашей стороны болгаро-экзархацкому ирредентизму вокруг Салоник, во всяком же случае, по крайней мере, пресечение потворства такому ирредентизму со стороны наших политических агентов.

7/ В виду той разбросанной группировки национальностей, которая существует в Македонской области, нет сомнения, что раздел ее на ‖ основании строго исключительно этнографических данных, был бы не л. 72 об. только затруднителен, но почти невозможен. Очевидно при таком разделе необходимо было бы принять в соображение и другие условия. Впрочем, нужно заметить, что по совершении раздела, последуюшая обоюдная трансмиграция для более сплошного сформирования националльных групп могла бы многое исправить. Такая трансмиграция не представляла бы ничего особенно нового на Балканском полуострове. Когда Берлинский трактат прирезал к Сербии участок турецкой территории с многочисленным албанским населением, Сербия не задумалась поголовно выселить в Коссовский вилает всех этих албанцев. После присоединения Восточной Румелии к Болгарии, мусульмане массами стали оттуда выселяться, а многочисленные македонцы переселялись в Болгарию. Из оккупированных провииций и теперь еще эмигрируют мусульмане, между тем как христианское население, несмотря на свои сетования, там остается.

В замечательной беседе, которую автор записки имел с г-ном Каллаи, незадолго до смерти этого выдающегося знатока балканских дел, правитель Боснии и Герцеговины выразил свое убеждение, что Коссово-Поле (старая Сербия) должно рано или поздно достаться в наследие сербскому королевству. Высказываясь в пользу такого аннексирования, г-н Каллаи
л. 73 однако заметил, что оно должно было бы иметь, в виду ‖ устойчивости нового устройства, непременным последствием трансмиграцию между албанцами, разбросанными островками до самой сербской границы и сербами, живущими среди албанцев вдоль албанской границы.

Без подобных последовательных трансмиграций после раздела, по мнению автора записки, вероятно было бы невозможно распутать гордиев узел македонской этнографии.

Изложив в семи предшествующих пунктах проект последовательного ряда мероприятий в виду достижения намеченного результата, автор записки поспешает оговориться в том смысле, что он отнюдь не считает такой проект единственно возможным. По его мнению, напротив того, *способы применения* следует признать настолько же *изменяемыми* и *разнообразными*, на сколько должна быть *неизменна и постоянна* раз установленная конечная цель.

A Tale of Two Artists: Valentin Serov and Leonid Pasternak

By RIMGAILA SALYS

1

THE Pasternak family collections in Oxford contain five drawings by Valentin Serov, including a hitherto unknown study for *Odysseus and Nausicaa*. These works, especially the *Odysseus and Nausicaa* study, contribute to our knowledge of the later years of Serov's artistic creativity. The circumstances in which they came to be in Oxford are part of the history of the long friendship between the Serov and Pasternak families, a friendship which ultimately found expression in Boris Pasternak's *Doktor Zhivago*.

Leonid Pasternak first met Serov during the mid to late 1880s, either in Munich, where Pasternak was then studying at the Academy, or in Odessa, when Serov went there to visit his future wife, Ol'ga Fedorovna Trubnikova.[1] Trubnikova was then head of the business office of the Odessa Imperial Music School (a branch of the St Petersburg Conservatoire), where Rozaliya Isidorovna Kaufman, Pasternak's fiancée, was a professor, and the women became friends without realizing that their future husbands were also acquainted.[2] The friendship continued when both couples settled in Moscow. Pasternak and Serov taught together at the School of Painting, Sculpture, and Architecture from 1897 until Serov's resignation in 1910. Rozaliya Isidorovna and Ol'ga Fedorovna met frequently and the two families became close. There were joint outings and the Pasternak children attended Christmas parties at the Serovs' in Muchnoi gorodok. These parties remained in Pasternak's memory and provided him with material for the Sventitsky Christmas party in *Doktor Zhivago*.[3]

The five works of V. A. Serov reproduced in this article are from the collections of C. A. Pasternak (Plates 1–3) and the Pasternak Trust (Plates 4–5). They are published by kind permission of the owners.

[1] O. F. Trubnikova (1865–1927) was an orphan brought up by Serov's relatives the Simonoviches. Leonid Osipovich himself could not remember exactly where he met Serov. See L. O. Pasternak, *Zapisi raznykh let*, ed. Zh. L. and A. L. Pasternak (M., 1975), 113–14; and idem, 'O Serove', in *Valentin Serov v vospominaniyakh, dnevnikakh i perepiske sovremennikov*, comp. and ed. I. S. Zil'bershtein and V. A. Samkov (L., 1971), i. 376, 378 n. 4.

[2] L. O. Pasternak, *Zapisi* (n. 1), 36–8.

[3] According to E. B. Pasternak in an interview with R. Salys in 1990.

Leonid Osipovich's recollections of Serov in *Zapisi raznykh let* are sympathetic and perceptive if somewhat partisan in dealing with World of Art,[4] a movement which Pasternak heartily detested after his clash with Benois in 1910.[5] Pasternak attributes the depression of Serov's last years both to his being trapped by the need to paint society portraits in order to support a large family[6] and to his association with World of Art, which made use of his reputation, though he had nothing in common artistically or socially with its members. Here Pasternak chooses to ignore Serov's work for Diaghilev, his friendship with Bakst, and the late, stylized classical line in his work which produced *The Rape of Europa*, *Odysseus and Nausicaa*, and *Portrait of Ida Rubinstein*. Serov's opinion of Pasternak's talent, on the other hand, was fairly objective. He considered him a master of children's portraits, but otherwise a portraitist of uneven achievement.[7]

2

After Serov's sudden death in 1911 his family was left without means and lived under difficult conditions for many years. Late in 1926 Ol'ga Fedorovna wrote to Leonid Osipovich describing the state of her finances and her poor health. She asked for help in selling a Serov portrait (of herself as a young woman) in Germany.[8] Rozaliya Isidorovna summarized the subsequent events thus:

Папа тотчас же ответил и указал на Столк.,[9] как на единственно возможного (конечно под большим вопросом?) и посоветовал даже ей самой ему написать, чтобы он не подумал, что папа этим промышляет и вообще побоялся испортить, если это все пойдет через него, так как он с этим хамом в ссоре уже года два — Шура знает и расскажет.[10]

Ol'ga Fedorovna replied to Leonid Osipovich as follows:[11]

Finland. Kuokkala. Rauva Maksimovitsch[12] für Olga Serov.
14-I-27 г.

[4] L. O. Pasternak, *Zapisi* (n. 1), 113–33.

[5] See R. Salys, 'Boris Pasternak on Leonid Pasternak and the Critics: Two Early Texts', *Russian Language Journal*, xlii (1988), 147–68.

[6] On the portrait of A. V. Tsetlin, painted in 1909, Serov commented: 'Vot zhaba.' See L. O. Pasternak, *Zapisi* (n. 1), 130.

[7] Ibid. 118; Josephine Pasternak in an interview with R. Salys in 1988.

[8] Her letter to Leonid Osipovich is referred to in an undated letter from Rozaliya Isidorovna to her son Boris, written in late January or early February 1927 and now in the Pasternak Family Archives, Moscow (hereafter PA).

[9] This is the Stol'kind referred to below in Ol'ga Fedorovna's letter of 14 Jan. 1927. He is believed to have been an attorney. Leonid Osipovich had painted his portrait in 1920.

[10] Letter written in late January or early February 1927 (n. 8). Quotations from this and all other letters in this article are published with the kind permission of the owners.

[11] Her letter (now in PA) is reproduced faithfully, including its idiosyncratic mixture of the old and new orthographies.

[12] This individual has not been identified.

Дорогой, милый Леонидъ Осиповичъ!

Спасибо Вамъ за письмо, очень за него благодарна и очень была ему рада. Поздравляю и я Вас и Розалію Сидоровну и Лидочку[13] с Новымъ годомъ и отъ всей души желаю побольше всемъ Вамъ здоровья и всего самого лучшаго дай Бог! Главное здоровье, теперь, когда я такъ мучаюсь, глубоко сознаю, что значитъ быть здоровой. Все это время не могла Вамъ ответить, очень скверно себя чувствовала, очень болела желудкомь, такъ мучили меня боли, кот. продолжаются по нѣсколько часовъ. Бедная Розалия Сидоровна тоже не ахти какъ здорова.[14] Господи, как я хочу съ Вами повидаться, ужасно, ужасно! Очень Вас люблю, какъ близких мне родныхъ, хоть-бы Богъ дал мне возможность добраться до Франции, но я что-то сомневаюсь, слишком слаба, вотъ напр. и раньше уже лежала и все праздники и новые и старые в постели провожу. Завтра жду изъ Выборга къ себѣ доктора. Пишу въ постели, м.б. неразборчиво, простите. Леонидъ Осиповичъ сегодня-же посылаю по Вашему совету послала сегодня письмо Столькинду, предлагая ему свой портретъ [15] за 1500 р. советскими деньгами, увы не знаю сейчас совсемъ, на Вас полагаюсь можете сбавить по своему усмотрению. Но вотъ въ чем дело, у меня с него нет фотогафии и сам портрет в Москве, но я надеюсь скоро его иметь у себя, а также м.б. получу и фотографии с него, просила снять.

Теперь, как мне быть? Я написала Столькинду, что могу портрет прислать в Берлин но еще не написала на что имя, когда буду его иметь у себя, но ведь придется пожалуй на Ваше имя послать и ему объ этомъ сообщить или какъ и что мне посоветуете м.б. другое.

Теперь, Леонидъ Осиповичъ я вздумала Вам послать рисунки В.А., м.б. кому ниб. продадите, а если не удастся, вернете мне их наложенным платежем. Цены я сообщу в следующем письме, если дорого — сами сбавьте, повторяю не знаю как сейчас оценить, Вамъ лучше знать, сами рѣшите, я с Вами буду согласна. А то я хвораю и мне крайне нужны деньги, а если поправлюсь, то на дорогу нужны, впрочем они всемъ нужны, что объ этомъ говорить. Пока до свидания. Больше не могу писать — устала. Очень цѣлую Розалию Сидоровну за письмо и прошу прощенія, что сейчасъ не могу ей ответить. Крѣпко жму Вам руку. Наташа проситъ очень поклониться. Будьте все здоровы.

Любящая Вас всех О. Сѣрова

Не знаете ли адресъ Грузенберга?[16]
и по новому и по старому пишу — все еще путаюсь.

[13] Lydia Pasternak Slater (1902–89), translator and poet, youngest daughter of Leonid Osipovich and Rozaliya Isidorovna.

[14] Rozaliya Isidorovna suffered from heart disease for much of her life.

[15] It is not clear which of several oil portraits of young Ol'ga Fedorovna is meant.

[16] Oskar Osipovich Gruzenberg (1866–1940), a well-known pre-revolutionary attorney. Serov painted a portrait of him and his wife Rosa Gavrilovna (d. 1942) in 1910, which is reproduced in *Valentin Serov: Paintings, Graphic Works, Stage Designs*, comp. with commentary by D. Sarabyanov and G. Arbuzov (New York and London, 1982), 356. The wealthy Gruzenbergs were living in Germany in the twenties. Ol'ga Fedorovna probably hoped to sell them some of her husband's works.

О «Похищении Европы» Я [*illegible word*] когда то не могла [*illegible word*] въ Мальме, нѣкот. шаги для продажи я предприняла. Цѣна 2,000 р. советских.[17]

Two or three days after receiving the letter the Pasternaks heard from D. S. Shor[18] that Ol′ga Fedorovna had died in Finland. A letter from Natasha Serova[19] followed:

Kuokkala.

3е Февраля
1927 г.

Многоуважемый Леонид Осипович!

Вы может быть уже прочли в газете, что моя мама скончалась здесь в Финляндии 18 го Января. Незадолго до своей смерти она послала Вам письмо в кот. пишет, что хочет Вам прислать на продажу папин эскиз к Навзикаи и рисунки. Я раньше послать не могла т.к. у меня было очень много дел и волнений в связи с похоронами. Посылаю Вам их только теперь. Значит один эскиз, на полотне и 14 рисунков: 9 натурщиц, 2 льва, головка дамская, Тришкин кафтан и запорожец.[20] Цены мама хотя и написала приблизительно в финских марках, но просила Вам передать, чтобы Вы, если найдется покупатель продавали-бы их за ту цену, кот. покажется Вам подходящей. Сама я думаю, что поеду в Париж к Юре[21] и если поеду, то скоро, т.к. он уезжает 15 го Февр. из Парижа на гастроли. На всякий случай я Вам напишу адрес нашего знакомого в Париже, куда можно писать и мне и Юре: Paris. Rue Wachington 9. Hôtel Modern. E. Grünberg[22] pour N. Séroff.

Уважающая Вас Наташа Серова

Pasternak resolved to find buyers for the drawings, although it would not be easy, as Rozaliya Isidorovna made clear to Boris:

Ты понимаешь, что здесь никто этим не интересуется из немцев, а русских охотников (?!) на это в настоящее время здесь нет, может разве в Париже, кроме того при жизни Ольги Феодоровны можно бы не «[*illegible word*]» разыграть и пр., а сейчас и эта возможность отпала. Конечно если они уже в

[17] *Pokhishchenie Evropy* (1910), tempera on canvas, 138 × 178 cm., Serov family collection, Moscow. Reproduced in *Valentin Serov* (n. 16), 205. It was shown at the 1914 Baltic Art Exhibition in Malmö, but was returned to the Serovs only in the summer of 1941. See O. V. Serova, *Vospominaniya o moem ottse Valentine Aleksandroviche Serove*, comp. with commentary by G. Arbuzov (L., 1986), 8. Ol′ga Fedorovna was obviously thinking of selling the painting abroad in 1927.

[18] According to Rozaliya Isidorovna Pasternak's undated letter to her son Boris, written in late January or early February 1927 (n. 8). The pianist David Solomonovich Shor (1867–1942), who taught at the Moscow Conservatoire from 1918 to 1925 and was a popular lecturer on music history for general audiences, is among the musicians depicted in Pasternak's *The Moscow Trio* (1917). He emigrated to Palestine in 1927 and corresponded with Leonid Osipovich for many years.

[19] Natal′ya Valentinovna Serova (1908–50), youngest of the six Serov children.

[20] The two lions must have been a lion and a tiger (see Plates 3 and 4). The works reproduced in Plates 1–5 are in the Pasternak family collections in Oxford. The other sketches sold in Germany have not come to light in the auction records examined.

[21] Georgy Serov (1894–1929), son of the artist, emigrated after 1917 and worked as an actor and film director in France.

[22] Serov was friendly with Yuly Osipovich Gryunberg, the business manager of the magazine *Niva*, and painted a portrait of his wife Mariya Grigor′evna in 1889 and his daughter Izabella in 1910.

пути, то делать нечего и папа приложит все старания, чтобы сделать что-нибудь — но если они еще не отосланы, то папа думает, чтобы ты (ведь у тебя ко всем есть доступ и мог бы от имени папы) на правительство повлиять насчет что мол позор упустить оставшиеся *последние* вещи этого великого художника и именно теперь когда она умерла (жена), а наследники может продадут частным лицам и пр. и пр.[23]

On her way to Paris, Natasha Serova stopped in Berlin on 13 April 1927 and delivered the drawings to Leonid Osipovich, together with a letter from Repin.[24]

Eventually Leonid Osipovich managed to sell almost all the Serov drawings and at higher prices than those named by Ol'ga Fedorovna. Those reproduced in Plates 1–3 were purchased by Fedor Pasternak, the husband of Josephine, Leonid Osipovich's elder daughter. That shown in Plate 4 was apparently bought by Leonid Osipovich himself. He noted that the last person to be offered the *Odysseus and Nausicaa* study (Plate 5) was Yakov Zakharovich Surits, the Soviet ambassador to Germany from 1934 to 1937.[25] Surits, however, was not interested and the work remained with Leonid Osipovich, who left Germany for England in 1938.

3

On the basis of style, the four pencil and black-chalk drawings (Plates 1–4) can be dated to the last ten years of Serov's life. He, like Leonid Osipovich, drew the human figure from life (Plate 1) whenever he had the opportunity, frequently working with his students at the School of Painting or with Mate's students in St Petersburg, and even abroad at the Julien Academy.[26] The shape of the nose, full lips, and sculpted eyelids in Plate 2 suggests that this drawing represents Ol'ga Fedorovna Serova.[27]

Serov was fascinated with animals all his life, and almost every one of his sketchbooks contains animal drawings. He sketched them in zoos at home and abroad as a respite from his portrait work.[28] In 1895 A. I. Mamontov conceived the idea of publishing an edition of Krylov's

[23] Letter written in late January or early February 1927 (n. 8).

[24] This short letter (published in I. Repin, *Izbrannye pis'ma v dvukh tomakh*, comp. I. A. Brodsky, ii (M., 1969), 396) recalls the success of Leonid Osipovich's *Resurrection* drawings at the 1900 Paris International Exhibition.

[25] Note written by L. O. Pasternak in 1943 (now in PA).

[26] I. Grabar', *Serov risoval'shchik* (M., 1961), 30–1. *Re* date of drawing in Plate 1, compare the male model (mistakenly entitled *Naturshchitsa*), 20 × 26 cm., in S. P. Yaremich, *Serov: Risunki* (L., 1936), unpaginated.

[27] Cf. *Valentin Serov* (n. 16), plate 26.

[28] Grabar', op. cit. (n. 26), 37. See also V. Derviz, 'Vospominaniya o V. A. Serove', *Iskusstvo*, 1934 no. 6, 122–3, and *Valentin Serov v vospominaniyakh* (n. 1), i. 210, 332–5, ii. 31.

fables with illustrations by Serov. The project never materialized, but the artist continued to work on the illustrations until the end of his life, especially during the last summer at Ino. Three days before his death he signed a contract for the publication of an edition of Krylov's fables with his illustrations.[29] While working on these illustrations, according to his relatives, he regularly drew on animal sketches made earlier, such as those reproduced in Plates 3 and 4. Lions, in particular, had always attracted him because of their interesting contours and proud bearing.[30]

Odysseus and Nausicaa belongs to the last period of Serov's work, from 1905 to his death in 1911, during which he was beginning to distance himself from the depiction of concrete, contemporary reality and was developing a monumental style in his portraits (such as *Ermolova*), historical subjects (such as *Peter I*), and classical subjects (such as *Odysseus and Nausicaa* or *The Rape of Europa*).[31] In 1903 he told Benois that he wanted to paint Nausicaa not as she was usually depicted, but as she really was.[32] His trip to Greece in 1907 deepened his interest in classical subjects and he began work on *Odysseus and Nausicaa* in 1909. According to Nikulina, he was attracted by the poetic quality of the story and the fact that it had been little used by artists.[33] His source is Book VI of the *Odyssey*, in which Odysseus is washed up on the shores of Scheria after years spent with the nymph Calypso. Inspired by Athena, the king's daughter Nausicaa goes with her serving women to wash clothes in pools near the sea. Odysseus hears the women's shouts as they toss a ball and he comes forward to ask for help. Nausicaa has him follow her home. 'While we go through the countryside and farmland / stay with my maids, behind the wagon, walking / briskly enough to follow where I lead.'[34] Serov thus chooses one of the happiest, most domestic episodes in the *Odyssey*. Unlike Bakst in *Terror antiquus*, he envisages a humane, noble, and elegantly simple Greece.

Apart from the Oxford study, there are seven extant versions of *Odysseus and Nausicaa*.[35] They are located as follows:[36]

[29] *Valentin Serov v perepiske, dokumentakh i interv'yu*, comp. with commentary by I. S. Zil'bershtein and V. A. Samkov (L., 1989), ii. 306–7.

[30] Grabar', op. cit. (n. 26), 40.

[31] D. V. Sarab'yanov, *Russkaya zhivopis' kontsa 1900-kh — nachala 1910-kh godov* (M., 1971), 20.

[32] S. Ernst, *V. A. Serov* (Spb., 1921), 67.

[33] N. M. Nikulina, 'Tema antichnosti v tvorchestve V. A. Serova "Odissei i Navzikaya"', in: *Antichnost' i sovremennost'*, ed. M. E. Grabar'-Passek *et al.* (M., 1972), 487. My commentary also draws from the following articles on this much-studied work: A. V. Bakushinsky, 'Formal'noe razreshenie motiva "shestviya" u Serova', in *Institut arkheologii i iskusstvoznaniya: Trudy sektsii iskusstvoznaniya*, ii (M., 1928), 198–212; N. Sokolova, '"Antichnyi tsikl" V. A. Serova', *Iskusstvo*, 1959 no. 8, 60–8; Sarab'yanov, *Russkaya zhivopis'* (n. 31), 31–2.

[34] Homer, *The Odyssey*, trans. Robert Fitzgerald (New York, 1963), 106.

[35] I. Grabar', *Valentin Aleksandrovich Serov: Zhizn' i tvorchestvo* (M., 1914), 294, also lists a watercolour in the E. M. Tereshchenko collection, St Petersburg, but I have not been able to locate this work.

[*See p. 81 for n. 36*]

(*a*) Gosudarstvennyi Russkii Muzei, St Petersburg (hereafter GRM), accession no. Zh-4298, tempera on cardboard, 49.5 × 65 cm.[37]
(*b*) Gosudarstvennaya Tret'yakovskaya Galereya, Moscow (hereafter GTG), accession no. 7866, tempera on cardboard, 85.5 × 101.5 cm.[38]
(*c*) GTG, accession no. 15787, watercolour and graphite, 19.9 × 27.7 cm.[39]
(*d*) Serov family collection, Moscow, watercolour and gouache on cardboard, 33 × 99 cm.[40]
(*e*) GTG, accession no. 1536, tempera on cardboard, 50.5 × 97 cm.[41]
(*f*) GRM, accession no. Zh-4288, tempera and pastel on paper, mounted on cardboard, 34 × 166.9 cm.[42]
(*g*) GTG, accession no. R-393, India ink and pencil on cardboard, 70.5 × 120 cm.[43]

In all eight versions the graceful Nausicaa with her lively mules (Serov the animal-lover preserves their characteristically twitching ears) and her 'gig / with pretty wheels and the cargo box upon it'[44] are the focus of attention. Odysseus is clearly secondary, although his figure gains interest as the composition develops in successive versions. Scholars have defined two stages in the evolution of the work. As originally conceived, the procession of vertically positioned figures moves against a high sky with prominent clouds. In (*a*), which may be the earliest version, a stylized Nausicaa has the ornate hair and familiar tunic of the Kore. The straight hair and close-fitting dress of all subsequent studies make her seem both more girlish and more real. The 'Karpovsky variant' (*b*) was painted at the Serov dacha in Finland and has a generally northern colouring, especially in the silvery blue water.[45] The last work in stage 1 is (*c*), in which Serov, while preserving the high sky and clouds of earlier variants, adds a lower horizon and the now firmly outlined figure of Nausicaa characteristic of stage 2. The stage 2 variants available in reproduction—(*e*), (*f*), and (*g*)—share the elongated picture-space characteristic of the decorative frieze and a

[36] The variants are listed in chronological order in so far as I have been able to establish this on the basis of Bakushinsky, 'Formal'noe razreshenie' (n. 33), Nikulina, 'Tema' (n. 33), and my own observations.
[37] Reproduced in *Valentin Serov* (n. 16), plate 200.
[38] Reproduced ibid., plate 201.
[39] Reproduced ibid., plate 198.
[40] No reproduction available. Location as given by Nikulina, 'Tema' (n. 33), 491.
[41] Reproduced ibid., facing p. 489.
[42] Reproduced in *Valentin Serov* (n. 16), plate 199.
[43] Reproduced in Nikulina, 'Tema' (n. 33), facing p. 489.
[44] Homer, *Odyssey* (n. 34), 101.
[45] Nikulina, 'Tema' (n. 33), 490.

directional tension between the vertical or right-sloping figure of Nausicaa, as she leans back to control her mules, and the leftward sloping figures of the serving women, Odysseus, and even the surrounding rocks.

The Oxford study appears to precede (*e*) chronologically and thus to be among the earliest works in stage 2.[46] Nausicaa and Odysseus are posed as in (*e*); the rock configurations on the right and left are the same, and to the right of Nausicaa the same outcropping is visible in the distance. At this point Serov makes Odysseus seem more thoughtful. He walks behind the lively Nausicaa with lowered head, as if reflecting upon his past and future. The northern colouring of stage 1 has been abandoned here for a more Mediterranean deep blue, now the dominant colour. All the elements of (*e*) and (*f*) are present in schematic form in the Oxford study. The fact that the latter is more elongated than any of the stage 1 variants typifies Serov's emphatic turn towards the frieze in stage 2.

4

The friendship between the younger generations of the Serov and Pasternak families continued after Serov's death and Leonid Osipovich's departure from Russia. In May 1947 at the Serovs' apartment Boris Pasternak gave a reading from the manuscript of *Doktor Zhivago* in memory of his childhood friend, the Serovs' eldest child Ol′ga, who had died the previous year.[47] Pasternak makes use in the novel of the location of the Serovs' apartment at the corner of Serebryanyi pereulok and Molchanovka. Stripped of its wooden fences and deserted between the two revolutions, the area has become unrecognizable. It now resembles a forest in which old women hunt for mushrooms. Zhivago meditates on the unexpected things that befall him there: 'Со мной там мимоходом всё неожиданности. То кого-нибудь встречу, кого двадцать лет не видел, то что-нибудь найду.'[48] It is there that he comes upon a man beaten by thieves, takes him to hospital, and looks after him, thereby gaining a powerful ally in the Soviet government who protects him for many years after. Here too, in the vestibule of the five-storeyed house at the corner of Serebryanyi and Molchanovka, he reads in the newspaper the announcement of the Bolshevik seizure of power and meets, but does not recognize, his half-brother Evgraf, who becomes his guardian angel for the rest of his life.

[46] Nikulina, 'Tema' (n. 33), 490.

[47] E. Pasternak, *Boris Pasternak: Materialy dlya biografii* (M., 1989), 592. O. V. Serova (1890–1946) is the author of *Vospominaniya o moem ottse Valentine Aleksandroviche Serove* (n. 17).

[48] B. Pasternak, *Doktor Zhivago: Roman. Povesti. Fragmenty prozy* (M., 1989), 189.

The street-names Serebryanyi and Molchanovka themselves bear upon a central theme in the novel—Zhivago's rejection of the revolutionary ethos in favour of authentic living. Instead of Strel'nikov's Roman virtue, the turmoil which sustains professional revolutionaries, and the new Soviet rhetoric, he embraces the everyday and the ordinary in which one can live, work, and create. After the February Revolution Zhivago works at a hospital in the Arbat district and frequents Serebryanyi and Molchanovka. During this time he is writing *Igra v lyudei*, a work arising out of his conviction that most people, like his friends Gordon and Dudorov, have stopped being themselves and are acting out some kind of life-role. The first decrees of the October Revolution, which Zhivago reads at the corner of Serebryanyi and Molchanovka, strike him as the only sincere words in a sea of hypocrisy: 'Какая великолепная хирургия! [. . .] Простой, без обиняков, приговор вековой несправедливости.'[49] By the time Zhivago is living at Varykino with his family, the revolutionary word has degenerated into a Soviet rhetoric which prevents him from living authentically: 'Что же мешает мне служить, лечить и писать? Я думаю, не лишения и скитания, не неустойчивость и частые перемены, а господствующий в наши дни дух трескучей фразы, получивший такое распространение, — вот это самое: заря грядущего, построение нового мира, светочи человечества.'[50] When Zhivago returns to Yuryatin after escaping from the Forest Brotherhood, he gets a haircut and shave from Glafira Tuntseva, as well as some proverbial advice which once again sends the reader back to Serebryanyi and Molchanovka: 'Да, стало быть, лучше никогда не говорить лишнего. Это истина вечная. Слово серебро, а молчание золото. [. . .] Лучше что-нибудь выдумайте, будто доктор или учитель. А что видов навидались, держите про себя.'[51] Tuntseva's words refer, of course, to the self-protective silence of the intelligentsia, people like the Serovs, Zhivagos, and Pasternaks, in a dangerous time. More importantly, however, she reminds Zhivago of his earlier resolve to reject the revolutionary word and, by implication, the revolutionary ethos in favour of authentic living. Glafira advises Zhivago (and the absent Lara) to become a doctor or teacher, i.e. to be themselves. As a member of the intelligentsia, Boris Pasternak is writing about himself here also. His correspondence makes this clear and adds another (in this instance literary) element to the Serebryanyi-Molchanovka nexus.

[49] Ibid. 196.

[50] Ibid. 280.

[51] Ibid. 376. For information on 'Slovo serebro, a molchanie zoloto', see V. P. Zhukov, *Slovar' russkikh poslovits i pogovorok* (M., 1966), 415. The proverb is also well known in other European languages. See Georg Büchmann, *Geflügelte Worte* (Berlin, 1905), 31–2, and Kurt Böttcher *et al.*, *Geflügelte Worte* (Leipzig, 1981), 235.

But it is not only Evgraf's steps that are heard in the house at the 'заколдованный перекресток'.[52] Remembering *A Tale of Two Cities*, Pasternak makes us hear the 'muffled tread' of fate, death, and history.[53] Dickens's Manettes, like the Serovs, live at an odd and fateful intersection; a corner building near Soho Square where 'forest trees flourished, and wild flowers grew' and 'mysterious backs and ends of houses peeped at them as they talked'.[54] Here Lucie listens to 'the echoes of all the footsteps that are coming by and by into our lives' and Sidney Carton hears the coming French Revolution, the 'great crowd bearing down upon us'.[55]

According to family sources, Pasternak read (or, more likely, reread) *A Tale of Two Cities* some time during the Civil War years, and it remained a favourite of his throughout his life. In late June 1921 Josephine Pasternak left Moscow and travelled to Germany to begin university studies in Berlin. It was she who initiated the events which changed the lives of the Pasternaks, parents and children, forever. Leonid Osipovich, Rozaliya Isidorovna, and Lydia followed in September. In a letter to Josephine, dated 21 July 1921, Boris sees through the prism of his beloved *Tale of Two Cities* the effect of her departure into a new life and the poetic sensibility breathing in her letters:

Ты помнишь, Люси, то место, где по поводу твоей поездки из города в город его прорывает в дилижансе несколько раз сряду фразою: «Возвращен, возвращается, возвращается к жизни».

Это ведь точка в точку та самая атмосфера чудесной сердечности (незаложенных ушей и снятого с трудпайка[56] воображенья-состраданья), de qua у нас с тобой res agitur. И вообще эта «Повесть», как она изумительным своим духом подыгрывает всему, что, пережив, ты заставила, — и это главное, — нас пережить. По своему, каждый из нас — доктор Манет. Папа и я прежде всего. Пассивный и величавый в своем неведеньи о собственном страданьи, величавый в своем беспомощном бесплодьи стук молотком по башмаку: у того — кистью по совпортрету, у этого пером по совстиху. По-своему Манеты и мама и Шура. Лида, кажется, по молодости — пощажена.

Что я под этим разумею? Механизацию привычки, низведенье профессии или семейной роли до шарниров умопомешательства, безмолвие мысли относительно заочного факта, превращающегося в пустое слово, бессердечную глухоту к его значенью. Или мы не знали, что было на тех полях и что это было в действительности? И вот, ты отымаешь у нас этот

[52] B. Pasternak, *Doktor Zhivago* (n. 48), 194.

[53] Charles Dickens, *A Tale of Two Cities* (London, 1960), ch. 1, p. 2.

[54] Ibid., ch. 6, pp. 86, 94.

[55] Ibid. 96. On Dickens and Pasternak, see Christopher J. Barnes, 'Pasternak, Dickens and the Novel Tradition', *Forum for Modern Language Studies*, xxvi (1990), 326–41.

[56] Boris viewed ration-cards as corrupting the fabric of society. See E. Pasternak, op. cit. (n. 47), 324.

злостный молоток из рук и выносишь за дверь привычную колодку. Произошло это не сразу. Прошла неделя и другая, пока сказалась твоя психиатрическая роль. Ко мне вернулся смех. Я опять знаю, что есть барьеры, которые существуют для того, чтобы оглянувшись по взятьи их, любоваться их низостью. Это ты несешь и сыплешь мне деньги. Если злостная тяга к молотку не одолеет старой башмачницы, мама проулыбается в этот период больше, чем за всю прочую Волхонку и часть Мясницкой.[57] Если тяга к колодке не повысит в глазах старого башмачника на минуту пошатнувшихся цен на «житейскую мудрость» и «здравый смысл», закон смертной угрозы, страхом коего направлялись все поступки и планы, уступит место законам живой веры в жизнь, которая так оказалась легка, прекрасна и надежна на твоем примере. Ах, дорогая моя, все это я уже знал раз и назвал это чудо. Это-то ведь и есть сестра моя жизнь.[58]

To survive and keep their sanity in Civil War Russia, father and son have taken up Soviet portrait painting and Soviet verse, in the same way that Dr Manette took up his hammer and scraps of leather in the Bastille. Facing starvation, Leonid Osipovich undertook various commissions for the Soviet government between 1919 and 1920.[59] Boris all but stopped writing between the latter half of 1918 and 1921. He did translations for Vsemirnaya literatura and the Theatre section of Narkompros. In autumn 1919 he had a position with the railway newspaper *Gudok* in which he himself wrote nothing, but corrected other people's verse 'and received a good Red Army ration for doing so'.[60] Finally, in June 1920 Boris was forced to ask the literary section of Narkompros for a food ration. He described the past seven months' work:

Это именно та степень напряжения, та форма и та каторжная обстановка работы, когда ее проводник и выполнитель, первоначально двинутый на зтот путь силою призванья, постепенно покидает область искусства, а затем и свободного ремесла и наконец, вынуждаемый обстоятельствами видит себя во власти какого-то непосильного профессионального оброка, который длится, становится все тяжелей и тяжелей и которого нельзя прервать в силу роковой социальной инерции.[61]

[57] The Pasternaks lived in apartments at the School of Painting, Sculpture, and Architecture in Myasnitskaya ulitsa from 1894 to 1911 and at Volkhonka no. 14 from 1911.

[58] Unpublished letter of 21 July 1921 from Boris Pasternak to Josephine Pasternak (in Josephine Pasternak Archives, Oxford). Cf. chs. 6 and 9 of *A Tale of Two Cities* (n. 53).

[59] They resulted in the production of the following paintings: *Praesidium of the Seventh Congress of Soviets* (1919), *Honour Guard at the Funeral of Ya. M. Sverdlov* (1919), *Praesidium of the All-Russian Central Executive Committee* (1920), *Lenin at the Second Congress of the Third International* (1920), *Lenin Speaking at the Plenum of the All-Russian Central Executive Committee* (1921), *Meeting of the Supreme Soviet of National Economy* (1921), *Lenin Speaking at an All-Russian Central Executive Committee Plenum* (1921).

[60] Letter of 19 Jan. 1921 from Boris Pasternak to D. Petrovsky, quoted in E. Pasternak, op. cit. (n. 47), 350.

[61] E. Pasternak, op. cit. (n. 47), 347.

Here was his Bastille, his hammer and bench. Finally, there was another 'old shoemaker', the gifted pianist Rozaliya Isidorovna, long imprisoned in her family role.

It is Josephine's openness to life, her determination to surmount the barriers of Soviet reality and look back on them from the vantage-point of her new life in Berlin, that takes the hammer and last away from Boris, Alexander, and their parents. Josephine ('Lucie') has cured them of the mechanical activities which they were forced to perform in order to survive in the prison of Soviet Russia. Once more they are ready to accept life; they no longer need to block it out by pounding their hammers. Josephine's letters reminded Boris of the miracle of 'my sister life', experienced and described in his *Sestra moya — zhizn'*. In early 1920 Pasternak wrote to Petrovsky that he had finally started writing again after a three-year hiatus.[62] During the summer of 1921 he met his first wife, Evgeniya Lur'ye.[63] Josephine's letters evoke another surge in the rising wave of his life.

Clearly the Manette paradigm was firmly planted in Boris Pasternak's consciousness, and he naturally returned to it when portraying the Revolutionary period in *Doktor Zhivago*. He chose the house at the corner of Serebryanyi and Molchanovka for the novel because the Serov family—so familiar to him in its traditions, values, and fate—represented the Pasternaks and all the other families of his circle who, like the fictional Zhivagos (and the Manettes before them), had been the accidental victims and sometimes beneficiaries of the configurations created at the crossroads of history.

[62] E. Pasternak, op. cit. (n. 47), 347.

[63] Ibid. 357.

APPENDIX

Specifications of Works Reproduced

Plate 1 *Female Model*
[1900s–1911] dated by style.
Black chalk on buff paper.
23.2 × 15.4 cm (exposed area).

Plate 2 *Woman in a Hat*
[1900s–1911] dated by style.
Black chalk on light brown paper.
15.7 × 13.8 cm (exposed area).
Signed l.r.: 'B'.
Inscribed l.r. with black ink stamp: 'BC' [B inscribed within the C].
Condition: foxing l.l., l.r. and scattered sparsely over picture area.

Plate 3 *Lions*
[1900s–1911] dated by style.
Pencil with faint traces of white chalk or pastel on yellow paper.
10.5 × 16 cm (exposed area).
Signed l.r: 'C'.

Plate 4 *Tiger*
[1900s–1911] dated by style.
Pencil with traces of white chalk or pastel on yellow paper.
11.7 × 18 cm (upper edge uneven).
Signed l.r.: 'B.C.'.
Verso inscribed u.r. in unknown hand: 400 мгр. фм.; inscribed l.r. by O.F. Serova: 'Удостоверяю рисунокъ В. А. Серова. О. Ф. Серова'.

Stored in a folder inscribed l.r. by L. Pasternak:
'рис. В. Серова Моя собственность Л. Пастернак'.

Plate 5 *Study for Odysseus and Nausicaa*
[1910] dated by the literature.
Tempera and charcoal on unstretched canvas.
63.5 × 172.1 cm (all edges uneven).
Signed l.r.: 'B.C.'.
Condition: fixative applied: nail holes all edges.

1. Valentin Serov, *Female Model*

2. Valentin Serov, *Woman in a Hat*

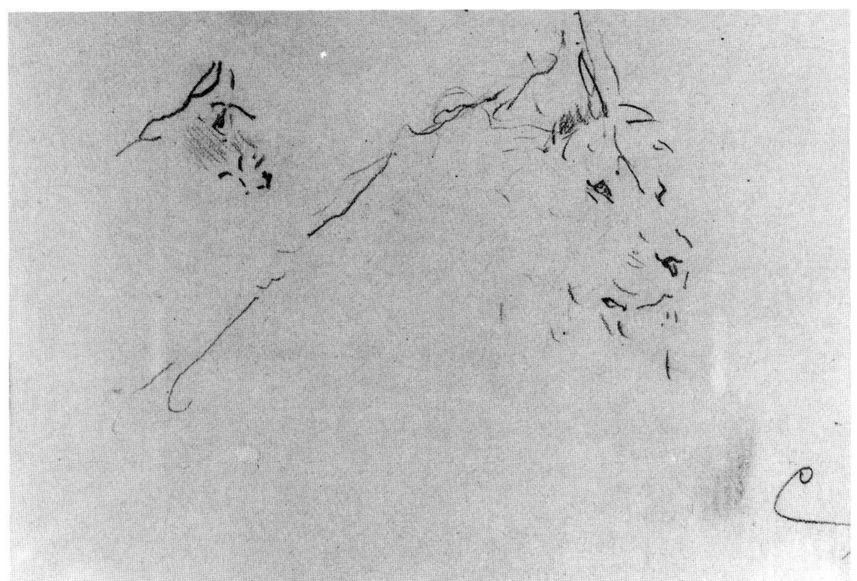

3. Valentin Serov,
Lions

4. Valentin Serov,
Tiger

5. Valentin Serov,
Study for *Odysseus and Nausicaa*

D. S. Mirsky to Maksim Gor'ky: Sixteen Letters (1928–1934)

By OL'GA KAZNINA *and* G. S. SMITH

THE biography of the critic D. S. Mirsky (Prince Dmitry Petrovich Svyatopolk-Mirsky, 1890–1939) is well known in broad outline,[1] but many particular episodes of it remain obscure. Of these episodes, Mirsky's decision to return to Russia in 1932 is perhaps the most significant. The letters of Mirsky to Maksim Gor'ky shed a good deal of light on this matter, and also on several other aspects of Mirsky's life and work at this crucial juncture. Certain short passages from these letters have been cited in existing work on Mirsky;[2] the full text of them is published here for the first time. The sixteen letters are preserved in the Gor'ky Archive of the Institute of World Literature, Moscow, nos. KG-II, 51-9-1 to KG-II, 51-9-17. What happened to Gor'ky's replies to Mirsky's letters is not known: it is likely that Mirsky either destroyed his archive when he left England, or that he took them with him to Russia and that, together with the letters he received after that date, they were seized when he was arrested in June 1937. It is conceivable that at least some of Mirsky's papers survive in the archives of the Soviet security services, but no evidence concerning this matter has been published to date.

Gor'ky and Mirsky first met personally when the latter travelled to Sorrento with his friend Petr Suvchinsky[3] in January 1928. Before this meeting, Mirsky had written a good deal about Gor'ky in various English-language publications. He unfailingly paid tribute to Gor'ky's creative talent, and recognized him as one of the greatest Russian

[1] See N. Lavroukine and L. Tchertkov, *D. S. Mirsky. Profil critique et bibliographique* (Paris, 1980); Gleb Struve, introduction to D. S. Mirsky, *Russkaya lirika. Malen'kaya antologiya ot Lomonsova do Pasternaka* (Paris, 1924; reprinted New York, 1979); M. Ya. Polyakov, 'Literaturno-kriticheskaya deyatel'nost' D. Mirskogo', in D. S. Mirsky, *Literaturno-kriticheskie stat'i* (Moscow, 1978), 5–18; N. Anastas'ev, 'Prisutstvie kritika', introduction to D. S. Mirsky, *Stat'i o literature* (M., 1987), 3–19; and G. S. Smith, 'D. S. Mirsky, Literary Critic and Historian', in D. S. Mirsky, *Uncollected Writings on Russian Literature*, ed. with an introduction by G. S. Smith (Berkeley, 1989) (referred to hereafter as *Uncollected Writings*), 19–43.

[2] Anastas'ev, 'Prisutstvie' (n. 1), 8.

[3] Petr Petrovich Suvchinsky (1890–1985) was a musicologist and a leading Eurasian. On his life, see Andrey Lishke, 'Konchina Petra Suvchinskogo', *Russkaya mysl'*, 21 Feb. 1985, no. 3557, p. 12; Vadim Kozovoï, 'Iz perepiski B. Pasternaka i P. Suvchinskogo', *Revue des études slaves*, lviii (1986), 637–9. See also idem, 'Perepiska B. Pasternaka i P. Suvchinskogo', ibid., lxii (1990), 727–82; Jury Kliukine, Vadim Kozovoï, and Lev Mnoukhine, 'Pis'ma M. I. Tsvetaevoi iz arkhiva P. P. Suvchinskogo', ibid. lxiv (1992), 183–221.

writers of his time. But Mirsky also paid considerable attention to the political and ethical positions that were stated or implied in Gor'ky's writings, eventually coming to the view that these aspects were more important than the artistic dimension: 'His articles, written since the beginning of the war and during the revolution, will prove perhaps a better claim to the attention of posterity than the romantic thieves and vagabonds of his earlier work.'[4] But in these views Mirsky pointed to a considerable element of ambiguity: 'Gor'ky, it is true, still holds our attention by his political (this is not quite the word) articles—cynical, incisive, extraordinarily perspicacious, but horribly distortive of Russian reality.'[5] And, perhaps most telling of all:

> With an enormous insight into reality, Gorki has no love of truth. And as he has no motive to restrain him from telling half-truths, and insinuating untruths, his essays more often than not become grotesque distortions of reality. This practically nullifies his moral weight in the eyes of all Russians. And it seems Gorki will be richly repaid for his contempt of the Russian people. Even now he is not taken seriously except by foreigners, for the Bolsheviks use him only as a convenient signboard to be contemplated from beyond the pale.[6]

Mirsky was inclined to take Gor'ky on trust when the latter was speaking of his 'genuine admiration for western culture', his 'barely concealed hatred for everything Russian', and his 'contempt' for Russia and the Russian *narod* (including the Bolsheviks). In one of his articles, Mirsky turns against Gor'ky the accusations made by the latter against the Bolsheviks: 'what is really Bolshevik in him is his genuine internationalism, his candid contempt for Russia, and his perfectly natural attitude towards the Russian nation, as only a material for universal "planetary" work—*Düngenvolk*, as the Germans put it.'[7] Here, Mirsky is following almost literally a statement by Gor'ky of December 1917.[8] The main reason for what he viewed as the savagery and ignorance, idleness and fatalism of the Russian people Gor'ky saw in the age-old yoke of orientalism, which was continued in the despotism of the Russian monarchy. While he had welcomed the revolutionary struggle against this element, and supported those aspects of it that in his view fostered the development of social ideals, Gor'ky could not accept the concrete forms taken by the Bolshevik stage in this struggle. In late 1917 and 1918 in his periodical *Novaya*

[4] D. S. Mirsky, 'A Russian Letter. Recent Developments in Poetry. Poetry and Politics', *The London Mercury*, iv (1921), 417. Republished in *Uncollected Writings*, 65.

[5] Idem, 'Russian Literature since 1917', *The Contemporary Review*, 1922 no. 680, pp. 205–11.

[6] Idem, 'The Literature of Bolshevik Russia', *The London Mercury*, v (1922), 277. Republished in *Uncollected Writings*, 70.

[7] Ibid.

[8] See *Novaya zhizn'*, 10 (23) December 1917, no. 198.

zhizn', Gor'ky repeatedly condemned the Bolsheviks and distanced himself from them.

It is remarkable, however, that Mirsky did not appear to take this anti-Bolshevik position seriously. As he saw it, Gor'ky occupied an exceptional position in revolutionary Russia: as a writer with a world reputation he belonged to the Bolshevik aristocracy. The criticism in *Novaya zhizn'* was particular and explicit, but it was aimed not at the idea of Bolshevism, rather at the way in which it was being implemented. Mirsky also emphasized that Bolshevism had not received any authentic expression in literature and that the writers who spoke in its name could only be called Bolsheviks in a conventional sense. 'For orthodox Bolshevism is an un-Russian and still more an un-intellectual movement. All the writers who are in some way or other connected with Bolshevism can be regarded as representative Bolsheviks only with the greatest limitations.'[9] 'Kindness had had to be sacrificed to progress, and the revolution in the name of kindness to be performed by means that were the negation of kindness. This is the source of Gorki's eternal perplexity, though he has done much to keep it undivulged.'[10]

In 1928, when these words were written, Gor'ky's situation was ambiguous: an idealogue of the new Soviet literature, he was living essentially in emigration. Although he carried a Soviet passport, his position was a source of incomprehension for both the opposed camps in Russian culture. He established cultural links between Soviet Russia and the Russian emigration, and for the West he symbolized Soviet literature. Mirsky called him 'our foremost living man of letters, the president, as it were, of the republic of Russian letters', and acknowledged 'his efforts to help his fellow-writers through the worst years of civil war and "war-time communism"'.[11]

Personal contact with Gor'ky made a tremendous impression on Mirsky, who several times testified that their meeting was a turning point in his life; in his autobiographical 'History of a Liberation' he stated:

The personality of Gorky, whom Suvchinsky and I visited in Sorrento, made a powerful contribution to my new education. Leaving aside the unforgettable impression made on me by the great charmer that was Gorky, this visit was our first direct contact with 'the other side of the barricade' and the first breath

[9] Mirsky, 'The Literature of Bolshevik Russia' (n. 6), 276. Republished in *Uncollected Writings*, 69.

[10] D. S. Mirsky, 'Contemporary Movements in Russian Literature', in: *Contemporary Movements in European Literature*, ed. W. Rose and J. Isaacs (London, 1928), 155. Reprinted in *Uncollected Writings*, 262.

[11] Ibid. 156. *Uncollected Writings*, 263.

of pure materialist air, coming from regions uninfected by the metaphysical miasma we had been breathing.[12]

Gor'ky had already heard of Mirsky as a result of watching developments in *émigré* literature. He had written a letter to A. K. Voronsky from Paris in 1926:

Здесь вышла первая книга журнала «Версты», очень толстая. Редактор — князь Святополк-Мирский [. . .] Он — очень умный и независимый критик, превосходно характеризовал Зайцева и Мережковского, Ходасевича и др. В журнале перепечатан Артем Веселый «Вольница», Бабель «Голубятня», Пастернак «Потемкин». Но тут же евразийцы, Лев Шестов, Артур Лурье и, конечно, Марина Цветаева с Ремезовым [*sic*]. Дело — княжеское.[13]

When they went to Sorrento in 1928, Mirsky and his friend Suvchinsky, as leading Eurasians at a critical moment in the evolution of that movement, were looking for Gor'ky's understanding and support.[14] In particular, they were about to launch the Eurasian newspaper *Evraziya*, and they probably intended to ask Gor'ky's advice about this undertaking, possibly with a view to securing distribution in the USSR. A detailed study of Eurasianism has yet to be made.[15] Relatively little is known in detail of Mirsky's part in the movement. He had become interested in it soon after he arrived in London in 1921, publishing two favourable articles.[16] Certain archival materials give

[12] Idem, 'Histoire d'une émancipation', *La Nouvelle Revue française*, xxxvii (1931), 392. Quoted here from the English translation in *Uncollected Writings*, 364.

[13] Letter of 24 July 1926 from A. M. Gor'ky to A. K. Voronsky, published in *Arkhiv A. M. Gor'kogo*, vol. 10: *M. Gor'ky i sovetskaya pechat'*, kn. 1 (M., 1964), 40.

[14] Suvchinsky in a letter to G. S. Smith dated 23 June 1974 stated: 'Я знал Горького еще в Петербурге-Ленинграде, познакомился с ним у Шаляпина. Д. П. [Мирский] не знал его и просил меня с ним познакомить. Я списался с Горьким и мы получили визы через поэта Унгаретти, что было в то время нелегко.' Suvchinsky told Veronique Lossky: 'Я часто встречал Горького в России, а потом в Сорренто. Мирский однажды попросил меня поехать с ним, и мы провели Рождество у Горького. Был такой поэт Магаретти [*sic*], он нам устроил визу, и мы поехали. За нами следили все время. Горький уговаривал нас ехать в Россию: «Я вас устрою», и он убедил Мирского и меня.' Veronika Losskaya, *Marina Tsvetaeva v zhizni* (Tenafly, 1989), 196.

[15] But see [H. N. Spalding], *Russia in Resurrection. A Summary of the Views and of the Aims of a New Party in Russia, by An English Europasian* (London, 1928); the British author and philanthropist H. N. Spalding (1877–1953) made financial contributions to the Eurasian movement. See A. V. Sobolev, introductory article to 'Polyusa evraziistva', *Novyi mir*, 1991 no. 1, p. 181. On Eurasianism, see also Otto Böss, *Die Lehre der Eurasier. Ein Beitrag zur russischen Ideengeschichte des 20. Jahrhunderts* (Wiesbaden, 1961); Nicholas V. Riasanovsky, 'The Emergence of Eurasianism', *California Slavic Studies*, iv (1967), 39–72; G. E. Orchard, 'The Eurasian School of Russian Historiography', in: Don K. Rowney and G. Edward Orchard (eds.), *Russian and Slavic History* (Columbus, Ohio, 1977), 97–105; Al'bert Sobolev, 'Knyaz' N. S. Trubetskoi i Evraziistvo', *Literaturnaya ucheba*, vi (1991), 121–30 (which contains the first published documentation of the penetration of the Eurasian movement by the Soviet security services; this penetration was alleged in A. B., 'Evraziitsy i "Trest"', *Vozrozhdenie*, 1953 no. 30, p. 126.). Cf. Vadim Kozhinov, 'Istoriosofiya evraziitsev', *Nash sovremennik*, 1992 no. 2, 140–67, which introduces a selection of articles by leading Eurasians (Savitsky, Suvchinsky, Trubetskoy).

[16] D. S. Mirski, 'The Exodus to the East', *Russian Life*, i (1922), 210–12; anon. [D. S. Mirsky], 'A "Eurasian" Manifesto', *The Times Literary Supplement*, 1 June 1922, p. 350. Suvchinsky stated: 'Я

more precise information. On 7 September 1922 Suvchinsky wrote to another prominent Eurasian, P. N. Savitsky:

В нашем полку прибыло. Вчера был у меня князь Святополк-Мирский, который в настоящее время читает лекции по истории русской литературы в Лондоне, и показал свою заметку в “Times” о евразийстве; он очень сочувствует всему движению [. . .] Постараюсь ближе его узнать.[17]

Six months later, Suvchinsky again writes to Savitsky, in an attempt to persuade the latter to publish an article on Russian literature by Mirsky in one of the Eurasian occasional collections:

Мирскому очень хочется печатно сочетаться со евразийством. Он просил меня передать Вам, что согласен на какую угодно редакторскую правку. [. . .] Это человек искренний и способный, его хорошо бы взять под свой «знак». Главное, он неистовый и стал ярым евразийцем, всюду проповедует! Подумайте еще о нем.[18]

In 1923 Suvchinsky charged Mirsky with organizing Eurasian activity in England, and in 1925 he informed Savitsky: ‘Евразийство растет: Мирский создал в Лондоне под своим руководством «местную группу евразийцев».’[19]

Mirsky in fact published only one article in the Eurasian series,[20] but he made many warm references to the movement in his publications.[21] The Journal *Versty* to which Gor'ky refers in the letter to A. K. Voronsky quoted above was edited by Mirsky together with two leading Eurasians, of whom Suvchinsky was one and Sergey Efron the other; there were in all three issues (1926–8). In 1927 Mirsky published what remained for many years the most substantial and authoritative survey of the movement.[22] In 1928 and 1929 Mirsky was a member of the editorial board of the Eurasian newspaper *Evraziya*, which was

познакомился с Д. П. Мирским в Берлине, в 1922 году, через Апухтина, кот. был того же полка (стрелок Е. В.), как и мы. Мирского заинтересовал сборник «Исход к Востоку», кот. был издан в Софии в 1921 году.’ (Letter to G. S. Smith, 23 June 1974 (n. 14)).

[17] Tsentral'nyi gosudarstvennyi arkhiv Oktyabr'skoi revolyutsii (TsGAOR), Moscow, *fond* 5783, *op.* 1, *ed. khr.* 388, *list* 26.

[18] Ibid., *list* 35. The article under discussion was not published; whether it has survived is not known.

[19] Ibid., *list* 57.

[20] ‘O moskovskoi literature i protopope Avvakume’, *Evraziiskii vremennik*, iv (1925), 338–50; reprinted in *Uncollected Writings*, 145–55.

[21] For example, ‘The literature of ideas has ceased to exist in Soviet Russia. It is quite alive among the *émigrés*, where the young generation, though failing to produce any important poetry or fiction, have given birth to the only significant post-revolutionary movement of ideas—the “Eurasian” movement.’ Mirsky, ‘Contemporary Movements’ (n. 10), 174. *Uncollected Writings*, 281.

[22] D. S. Mirsky, ‘The Eurasian Movement’, *The Slavonic Review*, vi (1927), 311–19; reprinted in *Uncollected Writings*, 237–45. In this article, however, Mirsky identifies the ideas of Eurasianism with those of Bolshevism and its economic programme to a greater extent than was acceptable for the founders of the Eurasian movement.

published in Clamart, the Paris suburb where Suvchinsky lived. Soon after the newspaper began publication, open discord broke out among the editorial board; the Paris members were politically more inclined towards the left than the Prague members. Savitsky regarded Suvchinsky and Mirsky as schismatics:[23]

Кламарские люди являлись теми, кому в 1927 г. были поручены сношения с пребывающими в Париже советскими гражданами и агентами советской власти. Вместо того, чтобы обратить этих людей в евразийство, сами кламарцы частично, или целиком перешли к коммунизму.[24]

Gor'ky's attitude towards Eurasianism was sceptical. He had written to I. M. Kasatkin in February 1926:

Есть такая секта эмигрантов, утверждающих, что Русь — не Европа, не Азия, а Евразия. Это несколько напоминает бездарнейшую болтовню Иванова-Разумника о Скифии. А недавно, в Праге «евразиец» Савицкий сделал доклад на тему, что текущая русская литература утверждает именно истины евразийства. И, представьте, он, отчасти, прав, хотя и глуп.[25]

In the second letter published below, Mirsky states that he has indeed become a Communist. Gor'ky asked his secretary P. P. Kryuchkov to find out what Mirsky needed to do in order to obtain a Soviet passport and visa. Kryuchkov replied: 'Мирскому необходимо подать заявление в ЦИК и пусть он через Вас перешлет просьбу в Москву.'[26] On 17 February 1931 Mirsky sent Gor'ky his statement to the Central Committee and on 31 July received the news from the Soviet consulate in London that his Soviet citizenship had been restored. But it is evident from the letters below that he was not at this time thinking of leaving his post at London University and Britain for good. By July 1932, however, he had no choice, as letter no. 12 makes clear. When Mirsky did eventually go back, Gor'ky became his principal contact and support in the process of entry into the Soviet literary world, and Mirsky participated in a number of projects associated with Gor'ky.[27] After Gor'ky's death in 1936, Mirsky no longer had a champion in his various disputes with the literary world, and less than a year later, on 4 June 1937, he was arrested, to die in a labour-camp near Magadan in January 1939.

[23] TsGAOR, Moscow, *fond* 5783, *op.* 1, *ed. khr.* 472, *list* 1.

[24] Ibid., *ed. khr.* 352, *list* 43-a.

[25] M. Gor'ky, *Pis'ma o literature* (M., 1957), 316.

[26] Letter dated 3 Feb. 1931. Institut mirovoi literatury (IMLI), Moscow, Arkhiv A. M. Gor'kogo, KG-P 41[a] 1/115.

[27] See G. S. Smith, 'An Annotated Bibliography of D. S. Mirsky's Writings, 1932–1937' in *Uncollected Writings*, 368–85.

1

17 Gower Street
London WC 1
2.2.28

Дорогой Алексей Максимович,
Я с отъезда все собираюсь писать Вам и все не могу найти подходящих слов, чтоб сказать, каким огромным благодеянием была для меня встреча с Вами.[28] Так вероятно и не найду, но у меня чувство, как будто бы я был не в Сорренто, а в России, и эта побывка в России меня страшно *выпрямила*. И нет наверно другого такого человека, который бы так носил в себе Россию так как Вы, и не только Россию, но и то, без чего Россия не может быть — человечество. Мне даже стыдно, что мы такими упырями сидели на Вас и пили эту Вашу русскую и человеческую кровь, и только уверенность, что ее в Вас хватит и на нас, позволяет не слишком каяться. Уходя от Вас, Сувчинский сказал мне: «А вот Толстого мы никогда не видели!» Только о Толстом мы и могли вспоминать. Но Вы более русский, больше «представляете собой» Россию, чем Толстой. Главное же я понял то чувство любви, которое так неизменно сохряняют все, видевшие Вас (по крайней мере кого я встречал). Простите, если пишу с чрезмерной (английской!) сентиментальностью. Но я не умею лучше выразить то чувство любви и благодарности, которыми Вы меня наполнили.

Д. С. Мирский

2

Постоянный адрес:
17 Gower Street
London WC 1
30.12.30

Глубокоуважаемый и дорогой Алексей Максимович,
я обращаюсь к Вам за советом и может быть за помощью. Когда три года тому назад я был у Вас, я был в самом начале той дороги, которая привела меня к полному и безоговорочному принятию коммунизма. Теперь — и уже не со вчерашнего дня — мое сокровенное желание посвятить какие у меня есть силы делу Ленина и Советских Республик. Психологические и бытовые трудности до сих пор мешали мне открыто сделать это. Я ждал выхода в свет моей книги (английской) о Ленине, которая позволила бы мне явиться не с совсем пустыми руками. Но выход этот задерживается по крайней мере до марта месяца, а время идет такое, что ждать нельзя.

[28] In a letter to Ol'ga Forsh of 6 Jan. 1928 Gor'ky writes that he has been visited by 'евразиец Сувчинский, проживающий в «Минерве» купно с одним из потомков Святополка Окаянного' and adds: 'Святополк Окаянный — бывший князь, спец по истреблению единокровных братьев.' *Gor'kii i sovetskie pisateli. Neizdannaya perepiska* (Literaturnoe nasledstvo, lxx) (M., 1963), 602. Svyatopolk 'the Accursed' was the murderer of his brothers, SS Boris and Gleb.

Процесс Промпартии, и гнусный лай, поднятый вокруг Ваших статей[29] буржуазной прессой, меня заставили с особой силой понять, что больше не может быть нейтралитета и половинчатости, и что кто не с рабочим классом — против рабочего класса. Я пишу к Вам прежде всего потому, что это самый естественный путь для интеллигента, даже если бы он и не был с Вами лично знаком, окончательно решающего стать на сторону коммунизма. Но также и потому, что более нормальный путь обращения в советское консульство не кажется мне вполне удовлетворительным, т. к. во-первых, меня двигает не советский патриотизм, а ненависть к буржуазии международной и вера в социальную революцию всеобщую; и во-вторых, что я совсем не хочу быть советским обывателем, а хочу быть работником ленинизма. Коммунизм мне дороже СССР.[30] Еще и потому я обращаюсь именно к Вам, что неизбежно бы отнеслись ко мне официальные советские власти с законным недоверием как к бывшему помещику и белогвардейцу. Я прошу Вас очень убедительно помочь мне, и сказать, что мне делать? Куда обратиться, чтобы с минимальной тратой времени я мог действительно и эффективно впрячься в дело, которое одно достойно человеческого достоинства. И еще разрешите прибавить, что за эти последние недели у меня не раз был прилив гордости за человечество (и за русское племя), что Вы есть на свете.

Глубоко уважающий и любящий Вас

Д. С. Мирский

3

17 Gower Street
London WC 1
18.1.31

Глубокоуважаемый Алексей Максимович,
большое спасибо Вам за Ваше письмо. Да, я понимаю, почему Вы из Италии ничего не можете сделать, и сам думал об этом прежде, чем писать Вам. Буду с надеждой ждать мая месяца. До этого должна выйти моя книга, на которую я возлагаю некоторые надежды в смысле облегчения всего этого. (А на днях посылаю Вам другую мою книгу — «Историю России» — хотя и очень плохую, оконченную два года тому назад, но только сейчас выходящую.)[31] Я очень буду рад написать статью, о которой Вы пишете, и постараюсь это сделать; боюсь только, что выйдет плохо, так как за это последнее время я потерял почти всякую связь с этой средой.
Еще раз большое спасибо за Ваше письмо.

Глубоко уважающий и любящий Вас

Д. С. Мирский

[29] This is a reference to Gor'ky's 'Otvet intelligentu'. See n. 35 below.

[30] Underlined thus by Gor'ky.

[31] This is Mirsky's *Russia. A Social History* (London, 1931). In the preface (p. ix) he states: 'The book was completed [. . .] in the spring of 1929 [. . .] I am fully conscious of grave defects in it, the most serious of which is the absence of a single point of view. This serious shortcoming is due to the fact that in the course, and under the direct action, of this work, my own historical conception underwent an adjustment [. . .].'

4

17 Gower St. London WC 1
17 февраля 1931 г.

Глубокоуважаемый и дорогой Алексей Максимович,
величайшее спасибо Вам за Вашу помощь и участие. Посылаю Вам, согласно Вашего письма, заявление в ЦИК, и на всякий случай короткие сведения о моем прошлом. Очень буду счастлив, если, как Вы говорите, можно будет уже поехать одновременно с Вами, в апреле месяце. Еще раз большое спасибо.

Глубоко уважающий и любящий Вас

Д. Мирский

5

University of London Club
17 Gower Street, WC 1
London
14.3.31

Глубокоуважаемый Алексей Максимович,
простите, что опять беспокою Вас. Очень уж томительно то состояние неизвестности, в котором я нахожусь. Нет ли у Вас утешительных новостей для меня?

Если бы не оказалось возможности получить разъяснения ко времени Вашей поездки, мне бы очень хотелось все-таки свидеться с Вами на Вашем пути в Москву. М[ожет] б[ыть] Вы остановитесь в Берлине? (Хотя М. И. Будберг,[32] которую я здесь видел, говорит, что вряд ли.) Во всяком случае, я собираюсь в Берлин во второй половине апреля.

Книга моя о Ленине[33] только что вышла и надеюсь, что Вы ее получили. На днях засяду за статью, о которой Вы мне писали.

Очень надеюсь на хорошие вести от Вас.

Глубоко уважающий и любящий Вас

Д. Мирский

[32] Baroness Moura Budberg (1893–1974) lived at one time in the Gor'ky household and translated Gor'ky's works into English. She wrote to Gor'ky on 14 Mar. 1931: 'Видела Мирского — он писал Вам? Его «Жизнь Ленина» на днях выходит. Он, кажется, твердо решил поехать в Россию, — Вы думаете это удастся? Кира ходит слушать его лекции в King's College, недавно он читал о Вас и Кира в своей тетради записала с его слов: «никто, никогда не произносил слово Человек так, как это сделал Горький.' IMLI, Moscow, Gor'ky Archive, KG-rzn 1-157/210. 'Kira' is Kira Arturovna Clegg, a Russian married to an Englishman. On Budberg's life, see Nina Berberova, *Zheleznaya zhenshchina* (New York, 1989) and the memoirs of Budberg's daughter, Tanya Alexander, *An Estonian Childhood* (London, 1989; first published as *A Little of All That*, London, 1987).

[33] This is Mirsky's *Lenin* (English edition, London, 1931; American edition, Boston, 1931). The article mentioned here would appear to be his 'Intelligentsiya i literatura Anglii. Iz doklada D. P. Mirskogo', *Literaturnaya gazeta*, 49 (218), 29 Oct. 1932, p. 4, which later was incorporated into his book *Intellidzhentsia* (M., 1934). The latter was published in an English translation by Alec Brown as *The Intelligentsia of Great Britain* (London, 1935).

6

c/o ml-le Mirsky
La Renaissance de l'Art
11 Rue Royale
Paris 8-e
30.3.31

Глубокоуважаемый Алексей Максимович,
меня очень смущает Ваше молчание. Я даже не знаю наверное, получили ли Вы заявление, которое я послал шесть недель тому назад. Мне тоже пришло в голову, что может быть мне нужно было послать особую просьбу об амнистии как бывшему белогвардейцу?

Я в Париже на неопределенное время. Неужели ничего не может выйти? Это было бы для меня катастрофично.

Глубоко уважающий Вас

Д. Мирский

7

Новый адрес: 7 Lansdowne Place
Brunswick Sq.
London WC 1
14.5.31

Дорогой Алексей Максимович,
я на днях, наконец, встретился с Сокольниковыми,[34] которые мне сказали, что были недавно у Вас в Сорренто и говорили с Вами обо мне. Он мне объяснил, что мое дело по самому существу не может не затянуться и обещал со своей стороны мне помочь. Я не волнуюсь (как Вы писали) и отношусь к этому вполне спокойно, тем более, что довольно неожиданно для меня я оказался вынужден предпринять довольно сложное и [*illegible word*] лечение, которое, я боюсь, затруднит для меня дальнейшее путешествие. С другой стороны, мне удалось наладить отношения со здешней партией, и вероятно удастся в ближайшем будущем с французской, и это уже очень меняет положение политического одиночества, которое меня так угнетало. Здешние коммунисты очень сочувственно отнеслись к моей книге о Ленине и даже в партийной печати очень ободряющие отзывы об ней. Но я до сих пор не знаю, как отнеслись к ней в Москве, а это для меня самое главное, прежде всего в смысле самопроверки.

[34] Georgy Yakovlevich Sokol'nikov (1888–1939) and his wife, the writer Galina Iosifovna Serebryakova (1905–80). From 1929 to 1934 Sokol'nikov was Soviet ambassador to Britain. In 1936 he was arrested. After serving less than three of the ten years to which he had been sentenced, he was shot. He was rehabilitated in 1989. Serebryakova, who had qualified as a doctor, was a prolific biographer and journalist. She published a book about England, *Очная ставка. Картины английской жизни* (M., 1933). Arrested in 1937, she spent 17 years in prison camps, but continued her literary career after her release.

Простите меня, если Вас затрудню еще одною просьбой. Во Франции есть (к сожалению совсем небольшая) группа бывших белогвардейцев, ныне рабочих, более или менее вполне принявших коммунизм. Конечно, они все очень стремятся домой, но я вообще им советую ориентироваться не на СССР, а на французскую партию, с которой их удалось связать, как будто (несмотря на естественное недоверие к ним французов). Теперь они меня запрашивают, можно ли им записаться на заочные курсы Заочного Коммунистического Университета при ЦК, чтобы таким образом ликвидировать свою политическую малограмотность. Согласится ли ЗКУ принять подписку на такие курсы б[ывших] белогвардейцев, живущих во Франции? Подчеркиваю, что они рабочие с большим стажем (5-8-10 лет) и субъективно вполне коммунисты.

До свидания, глубоко уважаемый и дорогой Алексей Максимович, помимо всего прочего ужасно хотелось бы Вас повидать и поговорить с Вами.

Д. Мирский

8

La Renaissance de l'Art
11 Rue Royale
Paris 8-e

Глубокоуважаемый и дорогой Алексей Максимович,
Вы меня, кажется, совсем забыли. Нет ли у Вас для меня какой-нибудь хорошей новости? Я знаю, впрочем, что Вы страшно заняты, особенно теперь, но Ваша доброта такая, что поневоле тянет ее эксплоатировать.

Я с величайшим вниманием и волнением читаю Ваши статьи,[35] и особенно Ваше письмо интеллигенту произвело на меня сильнейшее впечатление. Мне кажется, что этими статьями и всей Вашей позицией Вы делаете такое огромное дело, что даже то очень большое дело, которое Вами делалось до сих пор, почти что затмевается. Именно то, что Вы говорите эти вещи, дает им огромное значение. Это значит, что окончательно наступило время, что вне генеральной линии ВКП и Коминтерна нет места для тех, кто не хочет быть врагом человечества и культуры. И я настаиваю на том, что дело Коммунизма окончательно и безоговорочно слилось в одно, что нет ни человека, ни культуры вне Коммунистической революции. Вы сильнейшим образом приближаете день окончательной победы. Мне кажется, что среди честных и мыслящих интеллигентов и здесь, в Англии убеждение это зреет.

Я это последнее время связался со здешней партией и начинаю работать с ней, пока преимущественно литературно. Это огромная перемена для меня — больше не чувствовать себя ни павой, ни вороной.

[35] Mirsky has in mind Gor'ky's 'Otvet intelligentu' published simultaneously in *Pravda* (21 May 1931, no. 138, p. 5, and 22 May 1931, no. 139, p. 3) and *Izvestiya* (21 May 1931, no. 138, p. 3 and 22 May 1931, no. 139, p. 2); collected in M. Gor'ky, *Publitsisticheskie stat'i* (L., 1931), 274–89. The article was also sent for publication in French in *Paix mondiale* (see *Letopis' zhizni i tvorchestva A. M. Gor'kogo*, iv (M., 1960), 117). It was addressed to the Western intelligentsia and set out to explain the difference between bourgeois and Soviet culture.

Но когда же мне можно будет увидеть общее социалистическое отечество?

Можно Вас затруднить еще одной просьбой — один мой хороший приятель, бывший белогвардеец, но теперь рабочий и почти совсем коммунист, Николай Вонифатьевич Афанасьев подал заявление о возвращении. Мне кажется, что он вполне заслуживает этого. Он большой работник (хотя и без квалификации, он полуинтеллигент из крестьян) и из него должен выйти хороший ударник. Нельзя ли помочь ему?

Глубоко уважающий Вас

Д. Мирский

9

La Renaissance
11 Rue Royale
Paris 8-e
31 июля 1931

Глубокоуважаемый и дорогой Алексей Максимович,
я пишу, чтобы благодарить Вас за Вашу помощь и заступничество. Я получил из Лондонского полпредства извещение, что я восстановлен в советском гражданстве. Консульство еще не получило официальной инструкции об этом, но это очевидно вопрос ближайшего будущего. Не буду Вам говорить о том, какая это для меня радость. Надеюсь иметь возможность выехать во второй половине августа, не позже первого сентября. Очень, очень надеюсь, что застану еще Вас в Москве. Мне очень нужно Вас видеть. Я был бы очень Вам благодарен, если бы Вы нашли время ответить мне, могу ли я надеяться застать Вас.

Глубоко уважающий и любящий Вас

Д. Мирский

10

Hotel Récamier
Place St. Sulpice
Paris 6-e
13 августа 31 г.

Дорогой Алексей Максимович,
спасибо большое за телеграмму. Боюсь однако, что я уже Вас в Москве не застану. Я слышал (из газет и от видевших Вас), что Вы нездоровы и скоро едете в Италию. Очень надеюсь, что Вам луше, но очень надеюсь и что Вы поедете туда, где Вам лучше для здоровья. Для всех нас гораздо важней, я думаю, чтобы Вы были здоровы, чем чтобы Вы были географически в Союзе, — а политически и исторически Вы всегда там.

А мне, боюсь, не удастся выехать так скоро как хотелось бы. Паспорт я все еще не получил, но по получении его то да се задержит еще настолько, что раньше второй декады сентября вряд ли справиться. Так что мой первоначальный план ехать и вернуться в Лондон к началу учебного года (началу октября) сорван. Вместе с тем выясняется, что по-видимому с советским паспортом меня обратно в Англию не пустят, и потому мне представляется моим долгом перед английскими товарищами побывать еще там и поработать сколько смогу, — м[ожет] б[ыть] пока меня не вышлют, и тогда уже ехать в Союз насовсем, как говорят у нас в Тифлисе. Но меня очень смущает все это — я не знаю, правильно ли я решаю — мне очень нехватает авторитетного партийного руководства. В Англии я чувствую, что могу и чем могу быть полезен, а в Союзе? Я ясно вижу, что к политической работе меня допустить нельзя, а интересует меня только политическая работа. Что мне делать?

Можно к Вам еще по одному поводу пристать? Дело идет о Сувчинском, который, как вы знаете, учится петь. Я в этом деле ничего не понимаю, но говорят (Прокофьев напр[имер]), что его голос будет первый в мире и затмит Карузо (он драматический тенор). Мне известно, что брать уроки за последние месяцы он мог только благодаря Вашей помощи, но теперь положение его еще ухудшилось: шесть недель тому назад ему делали операцию: вырезали злокачественный костный нарост на ступне (т[ак] ч[то] он еще и теперь ходит на костылях); на что у него ушло все то немногое, что у него было: перебивается он теперь исключительно помощью людей, у которых и у самих немного. Знаменитые музыканты — Стравинский, Прокофьев расхваливают его вовсю, но ни копейкой не помогают. Нет ли возможности что-нибудь для него сделать в Москве? Политически он человек надежный — как Вы знаете, в основном, мы вместе с ним шли и пришли к коммунизму (только в политике он путаник, а в музыке нет). Не подавал он заявления о гражданстве до сих пор, т[ак] к[ак] все хочет дождаться и явиться в Союз не с пустыми руками. Нельзя ли было бы ему устроить пособие какое-нибудь? или что-нибудь единовременно хотя бы? Учиться ему еще месяцев шесть — к весне он будет совсем готов и тогда он будет в состоянии воздать за все это сторицей. Но теперь у него буквально ни гроша, и из-за каких-нибудь нескольких сот рублей все может быть сорвано. Как Вы думаете, можно что-нибудь для него сделать?

Простите, что я так к Вам пристаю и с собой и с другими, когда у Вас и так столько на руках.

С глубоким уважением, любящий Вас

Д. С. Мирский

11

11 Rue Royale (Paris 8-e) или
40 Torrington Sq., London WC 1
11 сент. 31

Дорогой Алексей Максимович,
очень большое спасибо за письмо и за Сувчинского.[36] Очень буду рад приехать в Италию и ехать с Вами в Москву. Да пустят ли меня в Италию? И

[36] Suvchinsky stated: 'Я тоже подал прошение о визе. Странно, в один день с Мирским: он в Лондоне, я в Париже — о возвращении в Россию. Ему дали, а мне отказали. Это ведь был

очень все-таки досадно все откладывать поездку. Но думаю, что в Англии можно будет еще поработать. Там вдруг открылись такие перспективы, о которых еще три месяца назад можно было только гадать. Я еду туда на днях.

Простите, что еще пристаю к Вам со своей особой: думаете ли Вы, что можно было бы мне и что стоит предложить советскому издательству издать книжкой мои последние статьи по литературным вопросам? Их наберется с десяток. Но они все на разных языках и предварительно мне пришлось бы их переводить, чего не стоит делать, если дело заведомо нестоющее.

Очень надеюсь, что Вам лучше и совсем хорошо.

Глубоко уважающий и любящий Вас

Д. С. Мирский

Я просил послать Вам номер Nouvelle Revue Française (сентябрь) с моей статьей.

12

17 Gower St.
London WC 1
10 июля 1932

Дорогой Алексей Максимович,
в Москве ли Вы и будете ли там когда я туда приеду? Приехать собираюсь в последних числах августа. Я собирался поехать в Союз прошлым летом, как только получил паспорт, но выяснилось, что я не был бы обратно допущен в Англию, почему и пришлось отложить поездку на год. Этот год, мне кажется, я провел не без пользы, особенно для себя, так как впервые по-настоящему и активно соприкоснулся с рабочим движением.[37] Теперь я собираюсь переехать в Союз на житье, но не знаю, какую работу мне там могут дать. Думаю (и боюсь), что это может быть только преподавательская работа, которая меня не очень привлекает; менее всего меня привлекает быть профессором литературы, — уже лучше история (которой я последние годы занимался гораздо больше). А вопросы литературы, для человека органически еще не связанного с рабочим классом — самые трудные. Литература, мне кажется, есть самое органическое, интимное и непредвидимое выражение новой культуры социалистической и говорить об ней можно только из самого нутра рабочего класса и строющегося социализма. Я в этой области уже наделал ошибок (в печати и устно) и хотя и вижу ошибочность сию — альтернативы не вижу. Поэтому вообще говоря хотелось бы оставаться возможно дальше от литературы и преподавания литературы.

настоящий белогвардеец, он был начальником штаба дивизии, которая шла на Харьков. Социально мы были одинаковы. И вот ему дали, а мне отказали.' Losskaya, *Marina Tsvetaeva* (n. 14), 196.

[37] Mirsky joined the Communist Party of Great Britain in May 1931 and spoke at various meetings up and down the country. He described his conversion in 'Why I became a Marxist', *The Daily Worker*, 30 June 1931, p. 2; an expanded version of this statement appeared as 'Histoire d'une émancipation' (n. 12).

Относительно же истории я последнее время много думал о том, что Вы могли бы стать центром большой энциклопедической работы, рассчитанной не только на советского читателя, но и на рабочих капиталистических стран. Особенно я об этом думал в связи с чтением книги Уэллса[38] (разбор которой я готовлю), которая чрезвычайно, до странного даже, плоха и импотентна, но читается (здесь и в Америке) очень широко (и именно рабочими), потому что кто палку взял, тот и капрал: она отвечает очень настоятельной потребности и ее, мне кажется, было бы легко заменить, если бы за это взялась хорошая бригада историков и писателей. Я очень хотел бы Вашего руководства и указаний относительно моей работы в Союзе. Одновременно я пишу в Наркомпрос, могу ли я рассчитывать на преподавательскую работу (без нее, я боюсь, мне не обойтись). В письме моем я позволяю себе сослаться на Вас.

Очень надеюсь застать Вас в Москве. Если бы Вы уезжали около этого времени, я бы ускорил свой приезд.

Глубоко уважающий и любящий Вас

Д. Мирский

13

Ленинград
30.9.32

Глубокоуважаемый и дорогой Алексей Максимович,
я наконец в Ленинграде и надеюсь послезавтра (2-го октября) ехать в Москву. Очень обидно, что на несколько дней всего опоздал на Ваш юбилей. Очень надеюсь иметь возможность Вас скоро увидеть. Сегодня, проходя по улице, увидел картинку: Вас на рабочем собрании, которая мне необыкновенно живо Вас напомнила и особенно захотелось Вас видеть. Вы могли бы дать знать, могу ли я Вас видеть и [*illegible word*] на адрес: Кооперативного издательства иностранных рабочих, Никольская 7, так как где я буду жить, я еще не знаю.

Любящий Вас

Д. Мирский

14

Русиновская, 7, кв. 34. Москва
19 фев. 1933

Дорогой Алексей Максимович,
хочу опять надоедать Вам с просьбой о репатриации. Дело идет о Вере Александровне Сувчинской,[39] бывшей жене Сувчинского. Она мой очень

[38] H. G. Wells, *The Work, Wealth, and Happiness of Mankind* (London, 1932). Mirsky's review appeared as 'Mr Wells Shows His Class', *The Labour Monthly*, xiv (1932), 383–7.

[39] Vera Aleksandrovna Guchkova (Vera Traill, 1907–87) was married first to P. P. Suvchinsky and then to a British journalist working in Moscow who was killed in the Spanish Civil War. Mirsky proposed marriage to her in 1930, but was refused. She moved to Moscow in 1936 (when her father died) and stayed until 1937, when she returned to Paris. After being interned by the

близкий друг и ручаться за нее я могу как за самого себя. К сожалению, она не писательница и потому она не может дать такую оценку своим убеждениям, как мог я. Я думаю, впрочем, что возражений против нее не было бы, не будь тут очень серьезной беды — дело в том, что она дочь активного и известного контрреволюционера А. Гучкова. И хотя она с ним в открытой вражде, этот факт, конечно, должен ей очень повредить. Зато ей могут помочь ее английские и французские друзья, которых у нее много в партии и около партии. Можно Вас просить как-нибудь помочь ей в этом деле?

Мои дела здесь идут нормально и удовлетворительно. Работы очень много — главная — участие в переводе Ленина на английский язык. Это оставляет мне довольно мало времени для книги об Англии, которую я пишу и которая подвигается не так скоро, как следовало бы.[40] Много вижу Авербаха, которого я очень ценю. В апреле надеюсь месяца на два поехать в Среднюю Азию, чтобы написать об этом для англичан. На днях видел Вс. Иванова по возвращении из Сорренто. Когда Вы собираетесь к нам?

Простите, что беспокою этими письмами. С большим приветом,

Д. Мирский

15

2 мая 1933

Дорогой Алексей Максимович,
завтра уезжаю в Среднюю Азию — Ташкент (где у меня поручение по истории заводов от Авербаха) и Сталинабад с намерением дальше ехать на Памир. Еду с Бруно Ясенским,[41] а там, надеюсь, подъедет еще Луговской.[42]

Очень жалею, что не увижу Вас еще так долго и что Вы скажете на писательском съезде. Но надеюсь, что Вы останетесь в Москве на все лето. Только что закончил статью для 2-го альманаха о формализме; здесь, Вы знаете, идет большая война с формалистами и «западниками» и я пользуюсь моим знанием их первоисточников, чтобы с ними воевать. Боюсь только, что я залез в этой статье в слишком большие исторические дебри.[43]

С горячим приветом,

Д. Мирский

Nazis when they occupied France and later released, she came to England in 1941. Her memoirs, recorded in interviews with G. S. Smith, are kept in the Brotherton Library, University of Leeds. A good deal remains to be discovered about her activities, especially her connection with the Soviet intelligence service; on the latter, see Alen Brossa, 'Gruppovoi portret s damoi', *Inostrannaya literatura*, xii (1989), 226–49 (translation of Alain Brossat, *Agents de Moscou* (Paris, 1988)).

[40] This is his *Intellidzhentsia* (n. 33 above).

[41] Bruno Jasieński (1901–39), the Polish writer, who joined the Communist Party in 1925 and moved to Moscow in 1929 after the scandal connected with his novel *Je brûle Paris*; his later work includes the once well-known *Chelovek menyaet kozhu* (1932).

[42] Vladimir Aleksandrovich Lugovskoy (1901–57), the Soviet poet.

[43] The reference is to D. Mirsky, 'O formalizme', in *God shestnadtsatyi. Al'manakh vtoroi* (M., 1933), 490–517. For a summary, see *Uncollected Articles*, 370.

16

9 марта 1934

Дорогой Алексей Максимович,
простите, что я опять беспокою Вас просьбой за одного из моих зарубежных друзей. Дело идет об Эмилии Эмануиловне Литауэр старой участнице всех наших с Сувчинским затей, а ныне деятельной работнице французского объединения революционных писателей (МОРП). Она в высшей степени ценный работник, с очень серьезной философской подготовкой (училась во Фрайбурге у Гуссерля), и последнее время пишет отличные статьи о фашистских философах во французском журнале Commerce. Но она совершенно погибает в Париже от безработицы, и с другой стороны от отсутствия соответствующей среды, которая могла бы ее по-большевистски руководить. Так как уровень ее марксистского развития такой, что ей там приходится выступать в учителях, что конечно ей не полезно. Она уже давно еще в 1932 возбудила ходатайство о возвращении. Казалось, что препятствий быть не должно: ее увезли родители из России девочкой лет 16; с ними (они коммерсанты) она давно порвала; ходатайство ее поддерживали члены ЦК французской партии (Ваян-Кутюрье). Между тем ей отказали. Прошлой осенью она возобновила ходатайство, а ответа все нет. По-видимому, задержка за какими-то ее однофамильцами, которые попались за нехорошие дела где-то на Украине. Мне доподлинно известно, что она ни с какими своими однофамильцами (кроме родителей и брата, с которыми она порвала) ничего общего не имеет и не имела. Я хотел бы иметь возможность дать показания об ней, чтобы рассеять это недоразумение. Я уверен, что она была бы здесь очень полезный человек и способствовала поднятию уровня нашей философской культуры. Она европеец в лучшем смысле слова и в то же время глубоко искренний, преданный коммунизму человек. Сделайте, дорогой Алексей Максимович, что-нибудь, чтобы спасти ее и доставить сюда![44]

Завтра утром я еду на Высокогорский рудник[45] работать над рукописью горняков (с опозданием, так как все это время болел). Как только вернусь, буду стараться Вас повидать.

Глубоко уважающий и любящий Вас

Д. Мирский

[44] Emiliya Litauer was repatriated to the USSR in 1936; she was arrested on 27 August 1939, interrogated about her contacts with the Paris Eurasians and particularly Sergey Yakovlevich Efron, and shot on 27 August 1941. Irma Kudrova, 'Poslednee "delo" Sergeya Efrona', *Zvezda*, x (1992), 129–30. Nikolay Vonifat'evich Afanasov (referred to as 'Afanas'ev' in letter 8 above) was repatriated in 1936, arrested on 29 January 1940, and shot on 27 July 1941. Ibid. 125, 129–30.

[45] Cf. D. Mirsky, 'O rudnike', in *Byli gory Vysokoi: Rasskazy rabochikh vysokogorskogo zheleznogo rudnika o staroi i novoi zhizni*, ed. M. Gor'ky and D. Mirsky (M., 1935), 10–20; this was the seventh volume in Gor'ky's series *Istoriya zavodov*.